DATE DUE

NOV 3 0 2022	

PRINTED IN U.S.A.

Blogs

Other Books in the Current Controversies Series

Blogs

Sylvia Engdahl, Book Editor

GREENHAVEN PRESS
A part of Gale, Cengage Learning

GALE
CENGAGE Learning™

Detroit • New York • San Francisco • New Haven, Conn • Waterville, Maine • London

Christine Nasso, *Publisher*
Elizabeth Des Chenes, *Managing Editor*

© 2008 Greenhaven Press, a part of Gale, Cengage Learning

Gale and Greenhaven Press are registered trademarks used herein under license.

For more information, contact:
Greenhaven Press
27500 Drake Rd.
Farmington Hills, MI 48331-3535
Or you can visit our Internet site at gale.cengage.com

For product information and technology assistance, contact us at

Gale Customer Support, 1-800-877-4253
For permission to use material from this text or product, submit all requests online at www.cengage.com/permissions

Further permissions questions can be emailed to permissionrequest@cengage.com

Articles in Greenhaven Press anthologies are often edited for length to meet page requirements. In addition, original titles of these works are changed to clearly present the main thesis and to explicitly indicate the author's opinion. Every effort is made to ensure that Greenhaven Press accurately reflects the original intent of the authors. Every effort has been made to trace the owners of copyrighted material.

LIBRARY OF CONGRESS CATALOGING-IN-PUBLICATION DATA

Blogs / Sylvia Engdahl, book editor.
    p. cm. -- (Current controversies)
    Includes bibliographical references and index.
    ISBN-13: 978-0-7377-3954-1 (hbk.)
    ISBN-13: 978-0-7377-3955-8 (pbk.)
    1. Blogs--Social aspects--United States--Juvenile literature. 2. Blogs--Political aspects--United States--Juvenile literature. 3. Online journalism--United States --Juvenile literature. 4. Freedom of speech--United States--Juvenile literature. 5. Blogs--Moral and ethical aspects--United States--Juvenile literature. I. Engdahl, Sylvia.
    HM851.B595 2008
    920--dc22

                                                          2008001712

Printed in the United States of America
3 4 5 6 7 12 11 10 09 08

Contents

Chapter 1: Are Blogs of Value to the Public?

Yes: Blogs Serve the Public in Ways Conventional Media Do Not

No: Blogs Offer Nothing Important to the Public at Large

Chapter 2: Do Blogs Have Significant Impact on American Politics?

Yes: Blogs Have Become Indispensable to Political Campaigns

Chapter 4: What Ethical and Legal Issues Are Raised by Blogs?

Foreword

By definition, controversies are "discussions of questions in which opposing opinions clash" (Webster's Twentieth Century Dictionary Unabridged). Few would deny that controversies are a pervasive part of the human condition and exist on virtually every level of human enterprise. Controversies transpire between individuals and among groups, within nations and between nations. Controversies supply the grist necessary for progress by providing challenges and challengers to the status quo. They also create atmospheres where strife and warfare can flourish. A world without controversies would be a peaceful world; but it also would be, by and large, static and prosaic.

The Series' Purpose

The purpose of the *Current Controversies* series is to explore many of the social, political, and economic controversies dominating the national and international scenes today. Titles selected for inclusion in the series are highly focused and specific. For example, from the larger category of criminal justice, *Current Controversies* deals with specific topics such as police brutality, gun control, white collar crime, and others. The debates in *Current Controversies* also are presented in a useful, timeless fashion. Articles and book excerpts included in each title are selected if they contribute valuable, long-range ideas to the overall debate. And wherever possible, current information is enhanced with historical documents and other relevant materials. Thus, while individual titles are current in focus, every effort is made to ensure that they will not become quickly outdated. Books in the *Current Controversies* series will remain important resources for librarians, teachers, and students for many years.

In addition to keeping the titles focused and specific, great care is taken in the editorial format of each book in the series. Book introductions and chapter prefaces are offered to provide background material for readers. Chapters are organized around several key questions that are answered with diverse opinions representing all points on the political spectrum. Materials in each chapter include opinions in which authors clearly disagree as well as alternative opinions in which authors may agree on a broader issue but disagree on the possible solutions. In this way, the content of each volume in *Current Controversies* mirrors the mosaic of opinions encountered in society. Readers will quickly realize that there are many viable answers to these complex issues. By questioning each author's conclusions, students and casual readers can begin to develop the critical thinking skills so important to evaluating opinionated material.

Current Controversies is also ideal for controlled research. Each anthology in the series is composed of primary sources taken from a wide gamut of informational categories including periodicals, newspapers, books, U.S. and foreign government documents, and the publications of private and public organizations. Readers will find factual support for reports, debates, and research papers covering all areas of important issues. In addition, an annotated table of contents, an index, a book and periodical bibliography, and a list of organizations to contact are included in each book to expedite further research.

Perhaps more than ever before in history, people are confronted with diverse and contradictory information. During the Persian Gulf War, for example, the public was not only treated to minute-to-minute coverage of the war, it was also inundated with critiques of the coverage and countless analyses of the factors motivating U.S. involvement. Being able to sort through the plethora of opinions accompanying today's major issues, and to draw one's own conclusions, can be a complicated and frustrating struggle. It is the editors' hope that *Current Controversies* will help readers with this struggle.

Introduction

The rise of blogging is an important development in the twenty-first century so far. Some believe it is a major revolution in human communication. In many situations—and certainly in nations where freedom of the press does not exist—it is having a major impact on the expression of public opinion. It has been hailed as a triumph of democracy because anyone with access to the Internet can start a blog, and it need not cost anything to do so.

But easy access with no start-up cost means that the sheer number of blogs as of 2007 was enormous. In October 2004, 4 million blogs worldwide were being tracked, over eight times as many as there had been in June 2003. A year later, there were over 19 million, and the number was doubling every five months. There were 57 million by October 2006, and 70 million by April 2007, when about 1.4 new blogs were being created every *second*.

To be sure, not all of those blogs are active, or even "real." Many people start blogs only to abandon them when they discover how much work and time it takes to keep writing. Some with a short-term reason for blogging never intended to continue, and still others simply run out of things to say. Furthermore, MySpace blogs comprise a sizable proportion of the total blog count, and because every MySpace profile includes blog space, users who post just a few times in it are included. In addition, fake blogs—spam blogs, known as splogs, which are created automatically by software that steals text containing popular keywords from other blogs—inflate the total, and it has been estimated that one out of five blogs is spam. Some sources estimate the figure of fake blogs as high as 56 percent.

Although splogs are a major problem for search engines such as Google, their large number does not make much difference when it comes to discovering blogs in which a person is potentially interested. Even half of 70 million is a lot of blogs; far more than any individual can visit and evaluate. Excluding foreign-language blogs does not help much either (although it leads to a huge reduction, since more blogs are written in Japanese than in English). There are not enough hours in a day for anyone to read more than a small fraction of the existing worthwhile blogs.

Of course, even avid blogging enthusiasts do not devote their full time to reading blogs. They have work to do and other activities that also demand their time. In his blog, businessman Fred Wilson wrote: "Most of us have day jobs. Many of us have families. So we have a limited amount of attention left. . . . So where does the attention come for the next wave of blogs and Web services? . . . So attention is a zero sum game and if we are creating (at an exponential rate?) more uses of attention, then we are facing a looming attention crisis."

Other bloggers agree with him. Jeff Nolan wrote: "My head is racked everyday attempting to keep up with 187 feeds [text input sent from blogs to be read on a single Web page] I'm tracking. I find myself reading feeds whenever I have as little as 2 minutes on the schedule and this jamming up is resulting in my having a lowered degree of comprehension about what I'm actually reading."

On top of the time they spend reading other people's blogs, serious bloggers must devote a lot of time to writing their own. Some maintain more than one blog. A Google search for the phrase "too many blogs" yields over 80,000 hits, and a good share of these refer to the problems faced by people who are trying to *write* too many. It is difficult to balance the time consumed by blogging between reading and writing, because the only way to attract new readers to a blog is to write comments about the posts in other blogs and to link to such posts.

Thus, as the blogosphere grows, some of the benefits it originally offered may evaporate. It is no longer possible for the average person to gain an audience simply through good writing, interesting ideas, and frequent posting. Although advice to new bloggers often implies that this is all it takes, in reality a well-written blog may never acquire more than a handful of readers apart from its author's friends. Well-established, popular blogs continue to gain readers from among people not already saturated with reading material, because these are the most prominent and therefore the most likely to be noticed. New blogs are likely to go unnnoticed. There are, of course, exceptions, but it cannot be said, as it once was, that blogging gives everyone a chance to communicate to the world at large.

The trend appears to be toward concentrating more and more information in fewer and fewer places, just as has happened with other media. Many widely read blogs representing various points of view will continue to be read. But professional bloggers—those who earn money from blogging in one way or another, whether as paid writers or by accepting advertising—may eventually overshadow amateurs. Whether the evolution will prove useful and valuable is debated. On one hand, amateurs often clutter the blogosphere with comments that are poorly written, trivial, and at times false or misleading. On the other hand, it is surely desirable for ordinary citizens to have an opportunity to express their ideas and to be heard.

CHAPTER 1

Are Blogs of Value to the Public?

Chapter Preface

To most teens, blogs are simply personal journals, a way of recording experiences and sharing them with friends. Indeed, millions of blogs of this kind are on the Web, maintained by people of all ages. But according to experts in communication, sociology, politics and business, what makes blogging a revolutionary cultural development is the way it has become a public-opinion shaping medium. The blogosphere (a term that refers collectively to all blogs and their interconnections) has become, as *Time* magazine put it, "a shadow media empire that is rivaling networks and newspapers in power and influence."

According to Technorati.com, the leading search engine for blogs, as of April 2007 there were over 70 million blogs worldwide, with about 120,000 new ones being added every day. Many of these blogs focus on their creators' personal lives and have only a few readers. However, other blogs address a wide range of subjects, from specialized hobbies to major political issues, and have large audiences. The most popular ones are read by hundreds of thousands. In fact, the mainstream media—newspapers, magazines, and TV networks—fear that their audiences will decline as more and more people turn to blogs for information, current news, and even entertainment. Some of the mainstream media have started their own blogs as a result.

Many bloggers consider themselves amateur or citizen journalists, and much discussion explores the possible impact of citizen journalism on democracy. Many commentators believe that the influence is definitely positive. In the past—at least the recent past—public opinion was formed by a few powerful entities such as network TV and big-city newspapers. No one else had an influential voice. With blogging, anyone can express opinions to the world at large, and writers who express themselves well gain attention. In nations where the government controls the press, the ability of bloggers to reach the public obviously leads to increased awareness of suppressed ideas. But even in the United States and other free nations, blogs give citizens a chance to be heard. They facilitate the discussion of controversial issues. Moreover, bloggers can expose errors in mainstream media coverage and cause those media to follow up on stories they might otherwise be inclined to drop or exclude.

Still, the readership of particular blogs is relatively small compared to traditional news sources, and this readership is polarized. Many people read only blogs that reflect their already-established convictions. Though many enjoy debate, they are not open to changing their views. So how much actual influence blogs have beyond providing opportunity for self-expression and/or contact with like-minded individuals remains to be determined.

In the early 2000s, a few prominent writers have expressed doubts about the advantages of the blog explosion; they argue that bloggers have neither the training nor the time to create work equivalent to that produced by professional journalists. Misinformation and rumor are spread by blogs as easily as is factual information, and telling the difference is all but impossible. Professional journalists strive, or at least claim, to be objective, whereas bloggers have the option of being as biased in their opinions as they want, sometimes to the extent of fanaticism. These and other criticisms are likely to increase as more people become aware of the blogosphere.

Whether or not the potential benefits hailed by blogging enthusiasts are realized, blogging appears to be here to stay. No one doubts that blogging is a major phenomenon in the early twenty-first century, but the precise nature and extent of its effect on American society is not yet known.

Blogs Give Citizens a Platform

Richard A. Posner

Richard A. Posner is a judge on the United States Court of Appeals for the Seventh Circuit, a senior lecturer at the University of Chicago Law School, and the author of many books. Along with the economist Gary Becker, he writes the Becker-Posner Blog.

The latest, and perhaps gravest, challenge to the journalistic establishment is the blog. Journalists accuse bloggers of having lowered standards. But their real concern is less high-minded—it is the threat that bloggers, who are mostly amateurs, pose to professional journalists and their principal employers, the conventional news media. A serious newspaper, like the [*New York*] *Times*, is a large, hierarchical commercial enterprise that interposes layers of review, revision and correction between the reporter and the published report and that to finance its large staff depends on advertising revenues and hence on the good will of advertisers and (because advertising revenues depend to a great extent on circulation) readers. These dependences constrain a newspaper in a variety of ways. But in addition, with its reputation heavily invested in accuracy, so that every serious error is a potential scandal, a newspaper not only has to delay publication of many stories to permit adequate checking but also has to institute rules for avoiding error—like requiring more than a single source for a story or limiting its reporters' reliance on anonymous sources—that cost it many scoops.

Blogs don't have these worries. Their only cost is the time of the blogger, and that cost may actually be negative if the blogger can use the publicity that he obtains from blogging to generate lecture fees and book royalties. Having no staff, the blogger is not expected to be accurate. Having no advertisers (though this is changing), he has no reason to pull his punches. And not needing a large circulation to cover costs, he can target a segment of the reading public much narrower than a newspaper or a television news channel could aim for. He may even be able to pry that segment away from the conventional media. Blogs pick off the mainstream media's customers one by one, as it were.

Bloggers Can Specialize

And bloggers thus can specialize in particular topics to an extent that few journalists employed by media companies can, since the more that journalists specialized, the more of them the company would have to hire in order to be able to cover all bases. A newspaper will not hire a journalist for his knowledge of old typewriters, but plenty of people in the blogosphere have that esoteric knowledge, and it was they who brought down [news anchor] Dan Rather [by uncovering the apparent forgery of documents he had called authentic]. Similarly, not being commercially constrained, a blogger can stick with and dig into a story longer and deeper than the conventional media dare to, lest their readers become bored. It was the bloggers' dogged persistence in pursuing a story that the conventional media had tired of that forced Trent Lott to resign as Senate majority leader.

The blogosphere has more checks and balances than the conventional media; only they are different.

What really sticks in the craw of conventional journalists is that although individual blogs have no warrant of accuracy, the blogosphere as a whole has a better error-correction machinery than the conventional media do. The rapidity with which vast masses of information are pooled and sifted leaves the conventional media in the dust. Not only are there millions of blogs, and thousands of bloggers who specialize, but, what is more, readers post comments that augment the blogs, and the information in those comments, as in the blogs themselves, zips around blogland at the speed of electronic transmission.

This means that corrections in blogs are also disseminated virtually instantaneously, whereas when a member of the mainstream media catches a mistake, it may take weeks to communicate a retraction to the public. This is true not only of newspaper retractions—usually printed inconspicuously and in any event rarely read, because readers have forgotten the article being corrected—but also of network television news. It took CBS so long to acknowledge Dan Rather's mistake because there are so many people involved in the production and supervision of a program like "60 Minutes II" who have to be consulted.

The Blogosphere Has Checks and Balances

The charge by mainstream journalists that blogging lacks checks and balances is obtuse. The blogosphere has more checks and balances than the conventional media; only they are different. The model is [economist] Friedrich Hayek's classic analysis of how the economic market pools enormous quantities of information efficiently despite its decentralized character, its lack of a master coordinator or regulator, and the very limited knowledge possessed by each of its participants.

The legitimate gripe of the conventional media is not that bloggers undermine the overall accuracy of news reporting, but that they are free riders.

In effect, the blogosphere is a collective enterprise—not 12 million separate enterprises, but one enterprise with 12 million reporters, feature writers and editorialists, yet with almost no costs. It's as if the Associated Press or Reuters had millions of reporters, many of them experts, all working with no salary for free newspapers that carried no advertising.

How can the conventional news media hope to compete? Especially when the competition is not entirely fair. The bloggers are parasitical on the conventional media. They copy the news and opinion generated by the conventional media, often at considerable expense, without picking up any of the tab. The degree of parasitism is striking in the case of those blogs that provide their readers with links to newspaper articles. The links enable the audience to read the articles without buying the newspaper. The legitimate gripe of the conventional media is not that bloggers undermine the overall accuracy of news reporting, but that they are free riders who may in the long run undermine the ability of the conventional media to finance the very reporting on which bloggers depend.

Some critics worry that "unfiltered" media like blogs exacerbate social tensions by handing a powerful electronic platform to extremists at no charge. Bad people find one another in cyberspace and so gain confidence in their crazy ideas. The conventional media filter out extreme views to avoid offending readers, viewers and advertisers; most bloggers have no such inhibition.

Lack of Filtering Does Little Harm

The argument for filtering is an argument for censorship. (That it is made by liberals is evidence that everyone secretly favors censorship of the opinions he fears.) But probably there is little harm and some good in unfiltered media. They enable unorthodox views to get a hearing. They get 12 million people to write rather than just stare passively at a screen. In an age of specialization and professionalism, they give amateurs a platform. They allow people to blow off steam who might otherwise adopt more dangerous forms of self-expression.

They even enable the authorities to keep tabs on potential troublemakers; intelligence and law enforcement agencies devote substantial resources to monitoring blogs and Internet chat rooms.

Blogs have exposed errors by the mainstream media that might otherwise have gone undiscovered or received less publicity.

And most people are sensible enough to distrust communications in an unfiltered medium. They know that anyone can create a blog at essentially zero cost, that most bloggers are uncredentialed amateurs, that bloggers don't employ fact checkers and don't have editors and that a blogger can hide behind a pseudonym. They know, in short, that until a blogger's assertions are validated (as when the mainstream media acknowledge an error discovered by a blogger), there is no reason to repose confidence in what he says. The mainstream media, by contrast, assure their public that they make strenuous efforts to prevent errors from creeping into their articles and broadcasts. They ask the public to trust them, and that is why their serious errors are scandals.

A survey by the National Opinion Research Center finds that the public's confidence in the press declined from about 85 percent in 1973 to 59 percent in 2002, with most of the decline occurring since 1991. Over both the longer and the shorter period, there was little change in public confidence in other major institutions. So it seems there are special factors eroding trust in the news industry. One is that the blogs have exposed errors by the mainstream media that might otherwise have gone undiscovered or received less publicity. Another is that competition by the blogs, as well as by the other news media, has pushed the established media to get their stories out faster, which has placed pressure on them to cut corners. So while the blogosphere is a marvelous system for prompt error correction, it is not clear whether its net effect is to reduce the amount of error in the media as a whole.

But probably the biggest reason for declining trust in the media is polarization. As media companies are pushed closer to one end of the political spectrum or the other, the trust placed in them erodes. Their motives are assumed to be political. This may explain recent Pew Research Center poll data that show Republicans increasingly regarding the media as too critical of the government and Democrats increasingly regarding them as not critical enough.

Competition in News Market Gives Consumers What They Want

Thus the increase in competition in the news market that has been brought about by lower costs of communication (in the broadest sense) has resulted in more variety, more polarization, more sensationalism, more healthy skepticism and, in sum, a better matching of supply to demand. But increased competition has not produced a public more oriented toward public issues, more motivated and competent to engage in genuine self-government, because these are not the goods that most people are seeking from the news media. They are seeking entertainment, confirmation, reinforcement, emotional satisfaction; and what consumers want, a competitive market supplies, no more, no less. Journalists express dismay that bottom-line pressures are reducing the quality of news coverage. What this actually means is that when competition is intense, providers of a service are forced to give the consumer what he or she wants, not what they, as proud professionals, think the consumer should want, or more bluntly, what they want.

Yet what of the sliver of the public that does have a serious interest in policy issues? Are these people less well served than in the old days? Another recent survey by the Pew Research Center finds that serious magazines have held their own and that serious broadcast outlets, including that bane of the right, National Public Radio, are attracting ever larger audiences. And for that sliver of a sliver that invites challenges to its biases by reading the *New York Times* and the *Wall Street Journal*, that watches CNN and Fox, that reads [conservative] Brent Bozell and [liberal] Eric Alterman and everything in between, the increased polarization of the media provides a richer fare than ever before.

So when all the pluses and minuses of the impact of technological and economic change on the news media are toted up and compared, maybe there isn't much to fret about.

Blogs Keep Watch over Mainstream Media

Daniel W. Drezner and Henry Farrell

Daniel W. Drezner is assistant professor of political science at the University of Chicago and keeps a daily blog at www.daniel drezner.com. Henry Farrell is assistant professor of political science and international affairs at George Washington University and a member of the group blog www.crookedtimber.org.

Every day, millions of online diarists, or "bloggers," share their opinions with a global audience. Drawing upon the content of the international media and the World Wide Web, they weave together an elaborate network with agenda-setting power on issues ranging from human rights in China to the U.S. occupation of Iraq. What began as a hobby is evolving into a new medium that is changing the landscape for journalists and policymakers alike. . . .

Blogs are already influencing U.S. politics. The top five political blogs together attract over half a million visitors per day. Jimmy Orr, the White House Internet director, recently characterized the "blogosphere" (the all-encompassing term to describe the universe of weblogs) as instrumental, important, and underestimated in its influence. Nobody knows that better than Trent Lott, who in December 2002 resigned as U.S. Senate majority leader in the wake of inflammatory comments he made at Sen. Strom Thurmond's 100th birthday party. Initially, Lott's remarks received little attention in the mainstream media. But the incident was the subject of intense online commentary, prodding renewed media attention that converted Lott's gaffe into a full-blown scandal.

Political scandals are one thing, but can the blogosphere influence global politics as well? Compared to other actors in

Daniel W. Drezner and Henry Farrell, "Web of Influence," *Foreign Policy*, November/ December 2004. www.foreignpolicy.com. Reproduced by permission.

world affairs—governments, international organizations, multinational corporations, and even nongovernmental organizations (NGOs)—blogs do not appear to be very powerful or visible. Even the most popular blog garners only a fraction of the Web traffic that major media outlets attract. . . .

Increasingly, journalists and pundits take their cues about "what matters" in the world from weblogs.

Blogging is almost exclusively a part-time, voluntary activity. The median income generated by a weblog is zero dollars. How then can a collection of decentralized, contrarian, and nonprofit Web sites possibly influence world politics?

Blogs are becoming more influential because they affect the content of international media coverage. Journalism professor Todd Gitlin once noted that media frame reality through "principles of selection, emphasis, and presentation composed of little tacit theories about what exists, what happens, and what matters." Increasingly, journalists and pundits take their cues about "what matters" in the world from weblogs. For salient topics in global affairs, the blogosphere functions as a rare combination of distributed expertise, real-time collective response to breaking news, and public-opinion barometer. What's more, a hierarchical structure has taken shape within the primordial chaos of cyberspace. A few elite blogs have emerged as aggregators of information and analysis, enabling media commentators to extract meaningful analysis and rely on blogs to help them interpret and predict political developments.

Blogs Are a Focal Point

Under specific circumstances—when key weblogs focus on a new or neglected issue—blogs can act as a focal point for the mainstream media and exert formidable agenda-setting power. Blogs have ignited national debates on such topics as racial profiling at airports and have kept the media focused on scandals as diverse as the exposure of CIA agent Valerie Plame's identity to bribery allegations at the United Nations. Although the blogosphere remains cluttered with the teenage angst of high school students, blogs increasingly serve as a conduit through which ordinary and not-so-ordinary citizens express their views on international relations and influence a policymaker's decision making. . . .

The blogosphere distills complex issues into key themes, providing cues for how the media should frame and report a foreign-policy question.

Most bloggers desire a wide readership, and conventional wisdom suggests that the most reliable way to gain Web traffic is through a link on another weblog. A blog that is linked to by multiple other sites will accumulate an ever increasing readership as more bloggers discover the site and create hyperlinks on their respective Web pages. Thus, in the blogosphere, the rich (measured in the number of links) get richer, while the poor remain poor.

This dynamic creates a skewed distribution where there are a very few highly ranked blogs with many incoming links, followed by a steep falloff and a very long list of medium- to low-ranked bloggers with few or no incoming links. . . .

Consequently, even as the blogosphere continues to expand, only a few blogs are likely to emerge as focal points. These prominent blogs serve as a mechanism for filtering interesting blog posts from mundane ones. When less renowned bloggers write posts with new information or a new slant, they will contact one or more of the large focal point blogs to publicize their posts. In this manner, poor blogs function as fire alarms for rich blogs, alerting them to new information and links. This self-perpetuating, symbiotic relationship allows interesting arguments and information to make their way to the top of the blogosphere.

For readers worldwide, blogs can act as the "man on the street," supplying unfiltered eyewitness accounts about foreign countries.

The skewed network of the blogosphere makes it less time-consuming for outside observers to acquire information. The media only need to look at elite blogs to obtain a summary of the distribution of opinions on a given political issue. The mainstream political media can therefore act as a conduit between the blogosphere and politically powerful actors. The comparative advantage of blogs in political discourse, as compared to traditional media, is their low cost of real-time publication. Bloggers can post their immediate reactions to important political events before other forms of media can respond. Speed also helps bloggers overcome their own inaccuracies. When confronted with a factual error, they can quickly correct or update their post. Through these interactions, the blogosphere distills complex issues into key themes, providing cues for how the media should frame and report a foreign-policy question.

Media Leaders Read Political Blogs

Small surprise, then, that a growing number of media leaders—editors, publishers, reporters, and columnists—consume political blogs. *New York Times* Executive Editor Bill Keller said in a November 2003 interview, "Sometimes I read something on a blog that makes me feel we screwed up."...

For the mainstream media—which almost by definition suffer a deficit of specialized, detailed knowledge—blogs can also serve as repositories of expertise. And for readers worldwide, blogs can act as the "man on the street," supplying unfiltered eyewitness accounts about foreign countries. This facet is an especially valuable service, given the decline in the number of foreign correspondents since the 1990s. Blogs may even provide expert analysis and summaries of foreign-language texts, such as newspaper articles and government studies, that reporters and pundits would not otherwise access or understand.

Blogs are now a "fifth estate" that keeps watch over the mainstream media. The speed of real-time blogger reactions often compels the media to correct errors in their own reporting before they mushroom.

Even foreign-policy novices leave their mark on the debate. David Nishimura, an art historian and vintage pen dealer, emerged as an unlikely commentator on the Iraq war through his blog, "Cronaca" which he describes as a "compilation of news concerning art, archaeology, history, and whatever else catches the chronicler's eye, with the odd bit of opinion and commentary thrown in." In the month after the fall of Hussein's regime in April 2003, there was much public hand-wringing about reports that more than 170,000 priceless antiques and treasures had been looted from the Iraqi National Museum in Baghdad. In response to these newspaper accounts, a number of historians and archaeologists scorned the U.S. Defense Department for failing to protect the museum.

Nishimura, however, scrutinized the various media reports and found several inconsistencies. He noted that the 170,000 number was flat-out wrong; that the actual losses, though serious, were much smaller than initial reports suggested; and that museum officials might have been complicit in the looting. "Smart money still seems to be on the involvement of Ba'athists and/or museum employees," he wrote. "The extent to which these categories overlap has been danced around so far, but until everything has been properly sorted out, it might be wise to remember how other totalitarian states have coopted cultural institutions, enlisting the past to remake the future." Prominent right-of-center bloggers, such as Glenn Reynolds, Andrew Sullivan, and Virginia Postrel, cited Nishimura's analysis to focus attention on the issue and correct the original narrative.

Blogs Compel Mainstream Media to Correct Their Own Errors

As the museum looting controversy reveals, blogs are now a "fifth estate" that keeps watch over the mainstream media. The speed of real-time blogger reactions often compels the media to correct errors in their own reporting before they mushroom. For example, in June 2003, the *Guardian* trumpeted a story in its online edition that misquoted Deputy U.S. Secretary of Defense Paul Wolfowitz as saying that the United States invaded Iraq in order to safeguard its oil supply. The quote began to wend its way through other media outlets worldwide, including Germany's *Die Welt.* In the ensuing hours, numerous bloggers led by Greg Djerijian's "Belgravia Dispatch" linked to the story and highlighted the error, prompting the *Guardian* to retract the story and apologize to its readers before publishing the story in its print version.

The more blogs that discuss a particular issue, the more likely that the blogosphere will set the agenda for future news coverage.

Bloggers have become so adept at fact-checking the media that they've spawned many other high-profile retractions and corrections. The most noteworthy was CBS News' acknowledgement that it could not authenticate documents it had used in a story about President George W. Bush's National Guard service that bloggers had identified as forgeries. When such corrections are made, bloggers create the impression at times that contemporary journalism has spun out of control.

Glenn Reynolds of "Instapundit" explained to the *Online Journalism Review* that he sees parallels between the impact of the blogosphere and Russia's post-Soviet glasnost. "People are appalled, saying it's the decline of journalism. . . . But it's the same as when Russia started reporting about plane crashes and everyone thought they were just suddenly happening. It was really just the first time people could read about them." Media elites rightly retort that blogs have their own problems. Their often blatant partisanship discredits them in many newsrooms. However, as Yale University law Professor Jack Balkin says, the blogosphere has some built-in correction mechanisms for ideological bias, as "bloggers who write about political subjects cannot avoid addressing (and, more importantly, linking to) arguments made by people with different views. The reason is that much of the blogosphere is devoted to criticizing what other people have to say."

The blogosphere also acts as a barometer for whether a story would or should receive greater coverage by the mainstream media. The more blogs that discuss a particular issue, the more likely that the blogosphere will set the agenda for future news coverage. Consider one recent example with regard to U.S. homeland security. In July 2004, Annie Jacobsen, a writer for WomensWallStreet.com, posted online a first-person account of suspicious activity by Syrian passengers on a domestic U.S. flight: "After seeing 14 Middle Eastern men board separately (six together, eight individually) and then act as a group, watching their unusual glances, observing their bizarre bathroom activities, watching them congregate in small groups, knowing that the flight attendants and the pilots were seriously concerned and now knowing that federal air marshals were on board, I was officially terrified," she wrote. Her account was quickly picked up, linked to, and vigorously debated throughout the blogosphere. Was this the preparation for another September 11-style terrorist attack? Was Jacobsen overreacting, allowing her judgment to be clouded by racial stereotypes? Should the U.S. government end the practice of fining "discriminatory" airlines that disproportionately search Arab passengers? In just one weekend, 2 million people read her article. Reports soon followed in mainstream media outlets such as NPR [National Public Radio], MSNBC, *Time*, and the *New York Times*, prompting a broader national debate about the racial profiling of possible terrorists. . . .

In all of these instances, bloggers relied on established media outlets for much of their information. However, blogs also functioned as a feedback mechanism for the mainstream media. In this way, the blogosphere serves both as an amplifier and as a remixer of media coverage. For the traditional media—and ultimately, policymakers—this makes the blogosphere difficult to ignore as a filter through which the public considers foreign-policy questions.

Blogs Are Emerging in Repressive Regimes

Blogs are beginning to emerge in countries where there are few other outlets for political expression. But can blogs affect politics in regimes where there is no thriving independent media sector?

Under certain circumstances, they can. For starters, blogs can become an alternative source of news and commentary in countries where traditional media are under the thumb of the state. Blogs are more difficult to control than television or newspapers, especially under regimes that are tolerant of some degree of free expression. However, they are vulnerable to state censorship. A sufficiently determined government can stop blogs it doesn't like by restricting access to the Internet, or setting an example for others by punishing unauthorized political expression, as is currently the case in Saudi Arabia and China. The government may use filtering technologies to limit access to foreign blogs. And, if there isn't a reliable technological infrastructure, individuals will be shut out from the blogosphere. For instance, chronic power shortages and tele-communications problems make it difficult for Iraqis to write or read blogs. . . .

The growing clout of bloggers has transformed some into "blog triumphalists." To hear them tell it, blogging is the single most transformative media technology since the invention of the printing press. Rallying cries, such as "the revolution will be blogged," reflect the belief that blogs might even supplant traditional journalism. But, as the editor of the Washington, D.C.–based blog "Wonkette," Ana Marie Cox, has wryly observed, "A revolution requires that people leave their house."

There remain formidable obstacles to the influence of blogs. All bloggers, even those at the top of the hierarchy, have limited resources at their disposal. For the moment, they are largely dependent upon traditional media for sources of information. Furthermore, bloggers have become victims of their own success: As more mainstream media outlets hire bloggers to provide content, they become more integrated into politics as usual. Inevitably, blogs will lose some of their novelty and immediacy as they start being co-opted by the very institutions they purport to critique, as when both major U.S. political parties decided to credential some bloggers as journalists for their 2004 nominating conventions.

Bloggers, even those in free societies, must confront the same issues of censorship that plague traditional media. South Korea recently blocked access to many foreign blogs, apparently because they had linked to footage of Islamic militants in Iraq beheading a South Korean. In the United States, the Pentagon invoked national security to shut down blogs written by troops stationed in Iraq. Military officials claimed that such blogs might inadvertently reveal sensitive information. But Michael O'Hanlon, a defense specialist at the Brookings Institution, told NPR that he believes "it has much less to do with operational security and classified secrets, and more to do with American politics and how the war is seen by a public that is getting increasingly shaky about the overall venture."

One should also bear in mind that the blogosphere, mirroring global civil society as a whole, remains dominated by the developed world—a fact only heightened by claims of a digital divide. And though elite bloggers are ideologically diverse, they're demographically similar.

Middle-class white males are overrepresented in the upper echelons of the blogosphere. Reflecting those demographics, an analysis conducted by Harvard University's Ethan Zuckerman found that the blogosphere, like the mainstream media, tends to ignore large parts of the world.

Nevertheless, as more Web diarists come online, the blogosphere's influence will more likely grow than collapse. Ultimately, the greatest advantage of the blogosphere is its accessibility. A recent poll commissioned by the public relations firm Edelman revealed that Americans and Europeans trust the opinions of "average people" more than most authorities. Most bloggers are ordinary citizens, reading and reacting to those experts, and to the media. As Andrew Sullivan has observed in the online magazine *Slate*, "We're writing for free for anybody just because we love it. . . . That's a refreshing spur to write stuff that actually matters, because you can, and say things you believe in without too many worries."

Blogs Provide Firsthand Information About the War in Iraq

Nikki Schwab

Nikki Schwab is a graduate student in journalism at American University in Washington, D.C.

When Capt. Danjel Bout lost three comrades in a single day while on an October 2005 mission in Baghdad, he stifled his grief and remained focused on what seemed to be the longest day of his life.

The next day, he let it out. He went to his computer and wrote a detailed and emotional account of the losses in his blog, "365 and a Wake up."

For Bout, blogging was a way to get some emotional relief from the hardships of war; it was an "online therapy session" of sorts. For the more than 750,000 viewers of his blog, it has been a way for them to read a firsthand account of the Iraq war according to Bout. "Anytime I think a story gets personalized, I think people can see the emotion behind the cold hard facts," the California Army National Guardsman said.

Soldiers Are Writing Blogs

Today, many of the stories coming from the wars in Iraq and Afghanistan are being written by those fighting them, in the form of thousands of soldiers' military blogs, or "milblogs." Their tales are unfolding as they occur, with limited censorship from the military, and they are attracting a growing readership from inside and outside the military.

Ward Carroll, the editor of military.com, an online military and veteran membership organization, said some of the best milbloggers have the ability to shape opinions on the war.

"If you are going to be informed, especially with something so controversial and polarizing as the Iraq war, you need to read one of these blogs along with the *Washington Post* and the *New York Times*," Carroll said.

Some prominent milbloggers started their sites to combat boredom during deployment or ease communication with family and friends at home, not expecting the blogs to become popular. Bout began his blog in 2005 because he was "too lazy to e-mail everyone individually" and filled it with candid descriptions of patrolling Baghdad's Dora neighborhood. During his 18-month deployment to Iraq, the officer lost 17 comrades. In his blog, he described how fallen soldiers were honored.

If you are posting information that you wouldn't tell someone face to face, why would you post it online?

Army Spc. Colby Buzzell began one of the first well-liked milblogs "My War: Killing Time in Iraq" in 2004 during month eight of his year-long deployment to Mosul. Buzzell said he read a *Time* magazine article titled "Meet Joe Blog" and it encouraged him to start blogging under the pseudonym CBFTW, an acronym standing for his initials and the tattoo on his arm, "[expletive] the world."

While Buzzell and Bout blogged from the frontlines, the military blogosphere is far more expansive. Pieced together, the milblogging community covers all aspects of modern military life. In addition to active duty soldiers, there are veterans like Matthew Currier Burden who run popular sites updating the community on the latest news from the war. Burden's blog "Blackfive" gets an average 20,000 views a day, though it sometimes spikes to over a million, according to Burden. There also are family members who blog, such as military wife Andi Hurley of the blogs "Andi's World" and "SpouseBUZZ," who discuss issues they face on the homefront.

The exact number of milblogs on the Internet is unknown. The *Mudville Gazette* hosts a Web ring of about 450 milblogs. Miblogging.com has more than 1,700 registered milblogs and an online subject search via Web clearinghouse Technorati shows more than 2,500 blogs on the military. These numbers continue to grow.

Blogs Have Been Censored for Security Reasons

Early in the Iraq war, the military shut down some milblogs over concerns that soldiers were violating operational security or OPSEC. Buzzell of "My War" wrote from June to September 2004, until he faced censorship and stopped blogging. Buzzell's witty and sarcastic entries on life as a machine gunner in Mosul gained him quick popularity. He believed superiors first became aware of the blog's existence after an entry was quoted in a newspaper account of an ambush.

Commanders told Buzzell what he could write about in his blog because they were concerned that he could endanger the mission. "I think I understand their concerns, you don't want Private Somebody over there releasing secrets or putting soldiers in jeopardy," Buzzell said.

After he continued posting, Buzzell was told that although he "wasn't being punished," he could not leave his base until "further notice," Buzzell wrote in his book "My War: Killing Time in Iraq." He told a *Wall Street Journal* reporter about his predicament. Once the reporter began to investigate, Buzzell said he was allowed to participate in missions again after about a week of being confined to his base. After this situation, he posted one blog entry that was pre-screened by his first sergeant. Then he decided to quit. "I knew subconsciously that if the Army found out, I would probably get in trouble," Buzzell said.

His scolding was minor compared to the punishment Jason Christopher Hartley received four months later, Buzzell said. Hartley authored the blog "Just Another Soldier," filling it with writings and dozens of pictures. Hartley posted graphic photos including one where troops set fire to a dead dog—"a common place roadside bombs are hidden," he wrote. He posted another of Iraqi children giving inappropriate gestures and a photo showing Hartley and a comrade sitting on the commode with their camouflage pants down.

Soldiers have the right to express themselves as long as they don't reveal information that will subject their unit or personnel to harm.

Hartley said his commander didn't appreciate his frank and sarcastic sense of humor. "In a way I kind of expected it," Hartley said. "I didn't expect the army—if they would find the blog—to have a sense of humor about it."

He said his platoon sergeant asked him to remove the blog as a favor. He did, but continued writing and e-mailed his stories to a list of interested readers. Near the end of his tour he republished the blog. It was discovered and Hartley, like Buzzell, was confined to his base for a month while an investigation was conducted. Hartley said he was told he had violated the Geneva Convention for posting pictures of detainees on the Internet. In addition, he was told he violated a direct order when he reneged on the promise to his platoon sergeant and republished the blog. His punishment was a $1,000 fine and a demotion.

Blogging Policies Take Shape

When Buzzell, Hartley and others began blogging from Iraq, there was no blanket Defense Department policy addressing the practice though there were policies prohibiting bloggers from revealing information about certain military activities, and policies that prevented them from blogging on military-owned computers. Lt. Gen. John Vines issued a blogging policy in April 2005 for coalition forces serving in Iraq. The policy required bloggers to register Web sites with their chain of command, and unit commanders were required to review these sites on a quarterly basis.

In August 2005, the mission of the Army Web Risk Assessment Cell was updated to include personal Web sites and blogs. This group of 10 Virginia Army National Guard members scours official government sites along with blogs by military personnel for OPSEC violations. Web pages and blogging now make OPSEC violations more serious because of the instantaneous nature of the medium and the global reach, wrote team leader Lt. Col. Stephen Warnock in an e-mail. His cell has examined thousands of blogs, and Warnock said he's seen improvement in the content of milblogs, with fewer items violating security.

The best way for bloggers to adhere to operational security is to use common sense, Warnock wrote. "If you are posting information that you wouldn't tell someone face to face, why would you post it online?" he wrote.

A recent policy change drew a negative reaction from one blogger. On April 19 the Army released an updated OPSEC policy, Army Regulation 530-1. This policy requires Army personnel to consult with a supervisor and their OPSEC officer before posting information in a public forum. This includes letters, e-mails, Web site postings and blog postings among other types of information, according to the policy. Burden, in a post on his blog "Blackfive," called the new policy "the end of military blogging." While Burden said he fears that this policy would impede Army members from blogging from war zones, Army OPSEC Program Manager Maj. Ray Ceralde, who helped author the revision, said bloggers shouldn't be concerned.

According to Ceralde, the new regulation does not require bloggers to have each post approved by officers, but rather instructs bloggers to alert commanders and OPSEC officers when they initially create a blog. This is similar to the policy already put in place in Iraq, he said. "Soldiers have the right to express themselves as long as they don't reveal information that will subject their unit or personnel to harm," Ceralde said.

Stifling bloggers could cause the most pro-military writers to stop posting because they are more likely to follow the rules, leaving only negative voices behind.

Dr. Leonard Wong, an associate research professor in the Strategic Studies Institute of the U.S. Army War College, said he believed the information on blogs could be used against American forces. "We have a very open society, and we are starting to realize that the enemy takes advantage of that," Wong said. While he couldn't cite a specific example of information from a blog being used against troops, he said the incident of Basra insurgents using Google maps to hit British military targets proves that they're capable of using information posted on the Internet in their attacks.

Rules for Bloggers Depend on Chain of Command

Most milbloggers that washingtonpost.com interviewed said censorship wasn't much of a concern, though the effects of the newest OPSEC policy have yet to be felt throughout the milblogosphere.

Burden of "Blackfive" said milbloggers have had different experiences because how closely the rules are followed depends on each blogger's chain of command. He is working to get policies loosened. He cautioned that stifling bloggers could cause the most pro-military writers to stop posting because they are more likely to follow the rules, leaving only negative voices behind. "Most of these people who are blogging are proud of what they do, and they volunteer to do this job. By and large they are a positive voice coming out of this war," Burden said. "You don't want to restrict them too much because they are providing a resource assisting what you are trying to do, which is winning the war."

He wants to see milbloggers who are blogging from the war zones given the same rules as embedded journalists. Bloggers from the home front already have started to receive privileges more closely aligned to those of professional journalists.

Roxie Merritt, the director of new media operations at the Office of the Secretary of Defense for Public Affairs, said while bloggers aren't being credentialed like media, the military is taking more time to communicate with bloggers to ensure that they post accurate information. She said the U.S. Central Command was the first command unit to reach out to bloggers. A command team was created to refer bloggers to information generally already available on one of the military's Web sites, according to Merritt. Since January, Merritt's office has hosted "blogger roundtables," which are conference calls for bloggers writing on Defense Department issues. Hurley of "Andi's World" and other milbloggers participate, posing questions to many top officials in the Multi-National Force of Iraq. . . .

For many milbloggers once their mission is completed, their blog is finished too. But this is not true for everyone. Buzzell and Hartley put portions of their blogs back online and wrote books based on their posts from Iraq.

Burden uses his blogging celebrity to raise money for the wounded. He raised $30,000 overnight for the family of a triple amputee so they could live in Washington while the soldier recovered at Walter Reed Army Medical Center. He also helped raise more than $210,000 in November 2006 to buy voice-activated laptops for soldiers with wounded hands.

He has no plans to stop blogging, though if he did, he said it would be for a good reason. "There's a lot of times when I think I would have been done a year ago because I thought this war would be over," Burden said. "I think that if I stopped blogging that would mean nobody else would be dying, so that would be a good thing."

Amateur Journalists' Blogs Spread Misinformation

Andrew Keen

Andrew Keen is an entrepreneur and author who is best known as a strong critic of the cultural impact of emerging Internet technologies. The following selection is from his controversial book The Cult of the Amateur: How Today's Internet Is Killing Our Culture *(2007).*

The "citizen journalists"—the amateur pundits, reporters, writers, commentators, and critics on the blogosphere—carry the banner of the noble amateur on Web 2.0. In fact, citizen journalism is a euphemism for what you or I might call "journalism by nonjournalists," or as Nicholas Lemann, Dean of the Columbia University Graduate School of Journalism, described them in the *New Yorker*: people who are not employed by a news organization but perform a similar function. Professional journalists acquire their craft through education and through the firsthand experience of reporting and editing the news under the careful eye of other professionals. In contrast, citizen journalists have no formal training or expertise, yet they routinely offer up opinion as fact, rumor as reportage, and innuendo as information. On the blogosphere, publishing one's own "journalism" is free, effortless, and unencumbered by pesky ethical restraints or bothersome editorial boards.

The simple ownership of a computer and an Internet connection doesn't transform one into a serious journalist any more than having access to a kitchen makes one into a serious cook. But millions of amateur journalists think that it does. According to a June 2006 study by the Pew Internet and

American Life Project, 34 percent of the 12 million bloggers in America consider their online "work" to be a form of journalism. That adds up to millions of unskilled, untrained, unpaid, unknown "journalists"—a thousandfold growth between 1996 and 2006—spewing their (mis)information out in the cyberworld.

Most amateur journalists are wannabe Matt Drudges—a pajama army of mostly anonymous, self-referential writers who exist not to report news but to spread gossip, sensationalize political scandal, display embarrassing photos of public figures, and link to stories on imaginative topics such as UFO sightings or 9/11 conspiracy theories. Drudge, who once wrote that "the Net gives as much voice to a thirteen-year-old computer geek like me as to a CEO or speaker of the House. We all become equal," is the poster boy of the citizen journalist movement, flashing his badge of amateurism as a medieval crusader would wield a sword.

Citizen journalists simply don't have the resources to bring us reliable news.

These four million wannabe Drudges revel in their amateurism with all the moral self-righteousness of religious warriors. They flaunt their lack of training and formal qualifications as evidence of their calling, their passion, and their selfless pursuit of the truth, claiming that their amateur status allows them to give us a less-biased, less-filtered picture of the world than we get from traditional news. In reality this is not so.

Blogs Spread Rumors

In 2005, in the aftermath of Hurricane Katrina, for example, many of the initial reports of the damage came from citizen journalists, people on the scene blogging about the chaos and taking photos of the devastation with their camera phones.

But, as it turned out, these initial reports helped to spread unfounded rumors—inflated body counts and erroneous reports of rapes and gang violence in the Superdome—that were later debunked by the traditional news media. The most accurate and objective reports instead came from professional news reporters who brought us high-quality photographs of the disaster and information from key figures like the New Orleans police, rescue workers, the U.S. Army Corps of Engineers, as well as first-hand accounts from the citizens and victims themselves.

Citizen journalists simply don't have the resources to bring us reliable news. They lack not only expertise and training, but connections and access to information. After all, a CEO or political figure can stonewall the average citizen but would be a fool to refuse a call from a reporter or editor at the *Wall Street Journal* seeking a comment on a breaking story.

One leading champion of citizen journalism, Dan Gillmor, author of the crusading *We the Media: Grassroots Journalism by the People, for the People*, argues that the news should be a *conversation* among ordinary citizens rather than a lecture that we are expected to blindly accept as truth. But the responsibility of a journalist is to inform us, not to converse with us.

If you simply want to converse with a journalist, invite them to your local bar for a few drinks. That's exactly what I did in the fall of 2006 when I spent an evening with Al Saracevic, deputy business editor of the *San Francisco Chronicle*.

Halfway through the evening, we got onto the subject of amateur journalism. "So what do you think distinguishes bloggers from professional journalists?" I asked him.

I'd expected Saracevic to focus on the quality of the end product. I expected him to tell me that amateur reporting on recent events like the 7/6 London bombings or New Orleans after Katrina wasn't up to real journalistic standards because it wasn't vetted by knowledgeable editors or wasn't corroborated by multiple sources. But I was wrong. While Saracevic might have agreed with the above, he had something else on his mind.

[Bloggers] aren't held accountable for their work in the way that real reporters are.

"In America, bloggers don't go to jail for their work," he told me. "That's the difference between professionals and amateurs."

Bloggers Are Not Held Accountable for What They Write

Saracevic was referring to Lance Williams and Mark Fainaru-Wada, his colleagues on the *Chronicle,* a two-person team of baseball reporters who had just been sentenced to eighteen months in prison for refusing to testify about the identity of the person who leaked them secret grand jury testimony from Barry Bonds.

In Saracevic's view, the blogosphere is a sideshow, all eyeballs and no real relevance, a poker game played with fake chips. Bloggers are very rarely sued or prosecuted because the government and corporations don't seem to really care what they write. As a result, they aren't held accountable for their work in the way that real reporters are.

In contrast, professional journalism matters. Companies sue newspapers, and reporters get sent to jail. Professional journalism is hardball. It counts—for the journalists, for corporations, for the government, and, most important, for all of us. This is because it is still only mainstream journalists and newspapers who have the organization, financial muscle, and credibility to gain access to sources and report the truth. As Saracevic later e-mailed me:

> It's as if libel law has taken a brief vacation so that citizen journalists can get their feet wet, while trashing the main-

stream media for "not speaking truth to power," as Craig Newmark puts it. Well, speaking truth to power takes money. Money to pay lawyers. Lots and lots of lawyers. Say what you will about the mainstream media, it takes big companies with a commitment to real investigative journalism to take on big institutions with any hope of surviving.

Amateur Journalists Are Self-Absorbed

Contrast this with another conversation I'd had, a few months earlier, with Dan Gillmor, the champion of citizen journalism I introduced earlier. I'd asked Gillmor what citizen journalism could provide that we can't get from mainstream media.

Gillmor's answer reflected the self-absorption of the typical amateur journalist. He told me that the real value of citizen journalism was its ability to address niche markets otherwise ignored by mainstream media.

The Internet is bloated with the hot air of these amateur journalists.

When I asked him for an example, he replied, hybrid cars. To him, proof of the value of citizen journalism was in news blogs about the Toyota Prius. Leave wars to the real reporters, he implied. The responsibility of amateurs was to report the latest feedback about the Prius. But is reporting about your favorite car really journalism? I asked him. According to Gillmor, it is.

> Is this journalism? I would say yes; it's a conversation, absolutely, but it's a collective bringing together of what people know, and when someone posts something that's not true, other people jump in and say well this is wrong.

In other words, professional journalists can go to jail for telling the truth: amateurs talk to each other about their cars.

Unfortunately, the Internet is bloated with the hot air of these amateur journalists. Despite the size of their readership, even the A-List bloggers have no formal journalistic training. And, in fact, much of the real news their blogs contain has been lifted from (or aggregated from) the very news organizations they aim to replace.

It is not surprising then that these prominent bloggers have no professional training in the collection of news. After all, who needs a degree in journalism to post a hyperlink on a Web site? Markos Moulitsas Zuniga, for example, the founder of Daily Kos, a left-leaning site, came to political blogging via the technology industry and the military. Glenn Reynolds, who leans to the right, was a law professor and an amateur music producer before jumping on his digital soapbox. Drudge was a mediocre student who came to the media business via a job managing the CBS studio gift shop. Such amateurs treat blogging as a moral calling rather than a profession tempered by accepted standards; proud of their lack of training, standards, and ethical codes, they define themselves as the slayers of the media giants, as irreverent Davids overcoming the news-gathering industry Goliaths.

Amateur Voices Distort the News

In the first Internet revolution, a Web site's value was determined by the number of eyeballs; in the Web 2.0 epoch, value is determined by its accumulation of amateur voices. In August 2006, I talked with digital media impresario Arianna Huffington (whose Huffington Post is one of the most highly trafficked blogs on the Internet), who boasted to me about ways in which her blog was planning to incorporate voices not traditionally heard in mainstream media. While papers like the *Los Angeles Times* or the *Washington Post* strive to maintain a singular, authoritative voice through the expert journalism they offer, Huffington claimed that her site was more truthful than traditional media because of its richer tapestry of amateur viewpoints. The problem is, these voices often distort the news, turning the music into noise (although as this book is going to press, Huffington is planning to add original reporting to her blog).

The *New Yorker*'s Lemann points out that "societies create structures of authority for producing and distributing knowledge, information, and opinion." Why? So that we know we can trust what we read. When an article runs under the banner of a respected newspaper, we know that it has been weighed by a team of seasoned editors with years of training, assigned to a qualified reporter, researched, fact-checked, edited, proofread, and backed by a trusted news organization vouching for its truthfulness and accuracy. Take those filters away, and we, the general public, are faced with the impossible task of sifting through and evaluating an endless sea of the muddled musings of amateurs.

Amateur journalism trivializes and corrupts serious debate.

Blogs on both the left and right have perfected the art of political extremism. Unlike professionally edited newspapers or magazines where the political slant of the paper is restricted to the op-ed page, the majority of blogs make radical, sweeping statements without evidence or substantiation. The most popular blogs are those that offer the seductive conspiracy theories and sensationalist antiestablishment platitudes that readers crave. As Lemann notes, even "the more ambitious blogs, taken together, function as a form of fast-moving, densely cross-referential pamphleteering—an open forum for every conceivable opinion that can't make its way into the big media, or . . . simply an individual's take on life."

The downside of all this "democracy," which the *Washington Post*'s Robert Samuelson described as the "greatest outburst of mass exhibitionism in human history," is the integrity of our political discourse. Amateur journalism trivializes and corrupts serious debate. It is the greatest nightmare of political theorists through the ages, from Plato and Aristotle to Edmund Burke and Hannah Arendt—the degeneration of democracy into the rule of the mob and the rumor mill.

Blogs Are a Threat to Intellectual Life

In 1961, Pulitzer Prize–winning playwright Arthur Miller wrote that "a good newspaper is a nation talking to itself." Fifty years later, in a nation where professional newspapers are losing readership to a seemingly endless stream of blogs and opinon-based sites, this conversation has taken a disturbing turn. Instead of starting our conversations about politics, economics, and foreign affairs from a common informed perspective, the amateur bloggers wax on trivial subjects like their favorite brand of breakfast cereal, or make of car, or reality television personality.

What Miller would see today in the Web 2.0 world is a nation so digitally fragmented that it's no longer capable of informed debate. Instead, we use the Web to confirm our own partisan views and link to others with the same ideologies. Bloggers today are forming aggregated communities of like-minded amateur journalists—at Web sites like Townhall.com, HotSoup.com, and Pajamasmedia.com—where they congregate in self-congratulatory clusters. They are the digital equivalent of online gated communities where all the people have identical views and the whole conversation is mirrored in a way that is reassuringly familiar. It's a dangerous form of digital narcissism; the only conversations we want to hear are those with ourselves and those like us.

Recently, Jürgen Habermas, one of Europe's most influential social thinkers, spoke about the threat Web 2.0 poses to intellectual life in the West. The price we pay for the growth in egalitarianism offered by the Internet is the decentralized access to unedited stories. In this medium, contributions by intellectuals lose their power to create a focus.

In this egalitarian environment, any intellectual—be it George Bernard Shaw, Ralph Waldo Emerson, or Habermas himself—is just another strident voice in the cacophony.

Most Blogs Reach Only Small, Specialized Audiences

Nicholas Lemann

Nicholas Lemann is dean of the Columbia University Graduate School of Journalism in New York City.

On the Internet, everybody is a millenarian. Internet journalism, according to those who produce manifestos on its behalf, represents a world-historical development—not so much because of the expressive power of the new medium as because of its accessibility to producers and consumers. That permits it to break the long-standing choke hold on public information and discussion that the traditional media—usually known, when this argument is made, as "gatekeepers" or "the priesthood"—have supposedly been able to maintain up to now. "Millions of Americans who were once in awe of the punditocracy now realize that anyone can do this stuff—and that many unknowns can do it better than the lords of the profession," Glenn Reynolds, a University of Tennessee law professor who operates one of the leading blogs, Instapundit, writes, typically, in his new book, *An Army of Davids: How Markets and Technology Empower Ordinary People to Beat Big Media, Big Government and Other Goliaths.*

The rhetoric about Internet journalism produced by Reynolds and many others is plausible only because it conflates several distinct categories of material that are widely available online and didn't use[d] to be. One is pure opinion, especially political opinion, which the Internet has made infinitely easy to purvey. Another is information originally published in other media—everything from Chilean newspaper stories and entries in German encyclopedias to papers presented at Micronesian conferences on accounting methods—which one can find instantly on search and aggregation sites. Lately, grand journalistic claims have been made on behalf of material produced specifically for Web sites by people who don't have jobs with news organizations. According to a study published last month [July 2006] by the Pew Internet & American Life Project, there are twelve million bloggers in the United States, and thirty-four per cent of them consider blogging to be a form of journalism. That would add up to more than four million newly minted journalists just among the ranks of American bloggers. If you add everyone abroad, and everyone who practices other forms of Web journalism, the profession must have increased in size a thousandfold over the last decade.

Citizen Journalism Is Not New

As the Pew study makes clear, most bloggers see themselves as engaging only in personal expression; they don't inspire the biggest claims currently being made for Internet journalism. The category that inspires the most soaring rhetoric about supplanting traditional news organizations is "citizen journalism," meaning sites that publish contributions of people who don't have jobs with news organizations but are performing a similar function.

What the prophets of Internet journalism believe themselves to be fighting against . . . is, as a historical phenomenon, mainly a straw man.

Citizen journalists are supposedly inspired amateurs who find out what's going on in the places where they live and work, and who bring us a fuller, richer picture of the world than we get from familiar news organizations, while sparing us the pomposity and preening that journalists often display. Hong Eun-taek, the editor-in-chief of perhaps the biggest citizen-journalism site, Oh My News, which is based in Seoul and has a staff of editors managing about forty thousand volunteer contributors, has posted a brief manifesto, which says, "Traditional means of news gathering and dissemination are quickly falling behind the new paradigm. . . . We believe news is something that is made not only by a George W. Bush or a Bill Gates but, more importantly, by people who are all allowed to think together. The news is a form of collective thinking. It is the ideas and minds of the people that are changing the world, when they are heard."

That's the catechism, but what has citizen journalism actually brought us? It's a difficult question, in part because many of the truest believers are very good at making life unpleasant for doubters, through relentless sneering. . . .

To live up to its billing, Internet journalism has to meet high standards both conceptually and practically: the medium has to be revolutionary, and the journalism has to be good. The quality of Internet journalism is bound to improve over time, especially if more of the virtues of traditional journalism migrate to the Internet. But, although the medium has great capabilities, especially the way it opens out and speeds up the discourse, it is not quite as different from what has gone before as its advocates are saying.

Societies create structures of authority for producing and distributing knowledge, information, and opinion. These structures are always waxing and waning, depending not only on the invention of new means of communication but also on political, cultural, and economic developments. An interesting new book about this came out last year [2005] in Britain under the daunting title *Representation and Misrepresentation in Later Stuart Britain: Partisanship and Political Culture.* It is set in the late seventeenth and early eighteenth centuries, and although its author, Mark Knights, who teaches at the University of East Anglia, does not make explicit comparisons to the present, it seems obvious that such comparisons are on his mind.

The "new media" of later Stuart Britain were pamphlets and periodicals, made possible not only by the advent of the printing press but by the relaxation of government censorship and licensing regimes, by political unrest, and by urbanization (which created audiences for public debate). . . . The most famous of the pamphleteers was Daniel Defoe, but there were hundreds of others. . . . These voices entered a public conversation that had been narrowly restricted, mainly to holders of official positions in church and state. They were the bloggers and citizen journalists of their day, and their influence was far greater (though their audiences were far smaller) than what anybody on the Internet has yet achieved.

You have to be very media-centric to believe that the press established the tone of national life rather than vice versa.

Pamphlets Had Great Influence

As media, Knights points out, both pamphlets and periodicals were radically transformative in their capabilities. Pamphlets were a mass medium with a short lead time—cheap, transportable, and easily accessible to people of all classes and political inclinations. They were, as Knights puts it, "capable of assuming different forms (letters, dialogues, essays, refutations, vindications, and so on)" and, he adds, were "ideally suited to making a public statement at a particular moment." Periodicals were, by the standards of the day, "a sort of interactive entertainment," because of the invention of letters to the editor and because publications were constantly responding to their readers and to one another.

Then as now, the new media in their fresh youth produced a distinctive, hot-tempered rhetorical style. . . . But one of Knights's most useful observations is that this was a self-limiting phenomenon. Each side in what Knights understands, properly, as the media front in a merciless political struggle between Whigs and Tories soon began accusing the other of trafficking in lies, distortions, conspiracy theories, and special pleading, and presenting itself as the avatar of the public interest, civil discourse, and epistemologically derived truth. Knights sees this genteeler style of expression as just another political tactic, but it nonetheless drove print publication toward a more reasoned, less inflamed rhetorical stance, which went along with a partial settling down of British politics from hot war between the parties to cold. . . . At least in part, Internet journalism will surely repeat the cycle, and will begin to differentiate itself tonally, by trying to sound responsible and trustworthy in the hope of building a larger, possibly paying audience.

Is the Internet a mere safety valve, . . . or does it actually produce original information beyond the realm of opinion and comment?

American journalism began, roughly speaking, on the later Stuart Britain model; during Colonial times it was dominated by fiery political speechmakers, like Thomas Paine. All those uplifting statements by the Founders about freedom of the press were almost certainly produced with pamphleteers in mind. When, in the early nineteenth century, political parties and fast cylinder printing presses developed, American journalism became mainly a branch of the party system, with very little pretense to neutral authority or ownership of the facts.

The U.S. Press Was Never in the Hands of a Few

In fact, what the prophets of Internet journalism believe themselves to be fighting against—journalism in the hands of an enthroned few, who speak in a voice of phony, unearned authority to the passive masses—is, as a historical phenomenon, mainly a straw man. Even after the Second World War, some American cities still had several furiously battling papers. . . . When journalism was at its most blandly authoritative—probably in the period when the three television broadcast networks were in their heyday and local newspaper monopoly was beginning to become the rule—so were American politics and culture, and you have to be very media-centric to believe that the press established the tone of national life rather than vice versa.

Every new medium generates its own set of personalities and forms. Internet journalism is a huge tent that encompasses sites from traditional news organizations; Web-only magazines like *Slate* and *Salon*; sites like *Daily Kos* and *News-Max,* which use some notional connection to the news to function as influential political actors; and aggregation sites (for instance, *Arts & Letters Daily* and *Indy Media*) that bring together an astonishingly wide range of disparate material in a particular category. The more ambitious blogs, taken together, function as a form of fast-moving, densely cross-referential pamphleteering—an open forum for every conceivable opinion that can't make its way into the big media, or, in the case of the millions of purely personal blogs, simply an individual's take on life. The Internet is also a venue for press criticism . . . and a major research library of bloopers, outtakes, pranks, jokes, and embarrassing performances by big shots. But none of that yet rises to the level of a journalistic culture rich enough to compete in a serious way with the old media—to function as a replacement rather than an addendum.

When one reads [blogs], after having been exposed to the buildup, it is nearly impossible not to think, This is what all the fuss is about?

The most fervent believers in the transforming potential of Internet journalism are operating not only on faith in its achievements, even if they lie mainly in the future, but on a certainty that the old media, in selecting what to publish and broadcast, make horrible and, even worse, ignobly motivated mistakes. They are politically biased, or they are ignoring or suppressing important stories, or they are out of touch with ordinary people's concerns, or they are merely passive transmitters of official utterances. The more that traditional journalism appears to be an old-fashioned captive press, the more providential the Internet looks. . . .

How Much Has Blogging Achieved?

Even for people who don't blog, there is a lot more opportunity to talk back to news organizations than there used to be. In their Internet versions, most traditional news organizations make their reporters available to answer readers' questions and, often, permit readers to post their own material. Being able to see this as the advent of true democracy in what had been a media oligarchy makes it much easier to argue that Internet journalism has already achieved great things.

Still: Is the Internet a mere safety valve, . . . or does it actually produce original information beyond the realm of opinion and comment? It ought to raise suspicion that we so often hear the same menu of examples in support of its achievements: bloggers took down the 2004 "60 Minutes" report on President Bush's National Guard service and, with it, Dan Rather's career; bloggers put Trent Lott's remarks in apparent praise of the Jim Crow era front and center, and thereby deposed him as Senate majority leader.

The best original Internet journalism happens more often by accident, when smart and curious people with access to means of communication are at the scene of a sudden disaster. Any time that big news happens unexpectedly, or in remote and dangerous places, there is more raw information available right away on the Internet than through established news organizations. The most memorable photographs of the

London terrorist bombing last summer were taken by subway riders using cell phones, not by news photographers, who didn't have time to get there. There were more ordinary people than paid reporters posting information when the tsunami first hit South Asia, in 2004, when Hurricane Katrina hit the Gulf Coast, in 2005, and when Israeli bombs hit Beirut [in summer 2006]. I am in an especially good position to appreciate the benefits of citizen journalism at such moments, because it helped save my father and stepmother's lives when they were stranded in New Orleans after Hurricane Katrina: the citizen portions of the Web sites of local news organizations were, for a crucial day or two, one of the best places to get information about how to drive out of the city. But, over time, the best information about why the hurricane destroyed so much of the city came from reporters, not citizens.

> *Most citizen journalism reaches very small and specialized audiences and is proudly minor in its concerns.*

Eyewitness accounts and information-sharing during sudden disasters are welcome, even if they don't provide a complete report of what is going on in a particular situation. And that is what citizen journalism is supposed to do: keep up with public affairs, especially locally, year in and year out, even when there's no disaster.... But when one reads it, after having been exposed to the buildup, it is nearly impossible not to think, This is what all the fuss is about?...

The Content of Most Blogs Is Trivial

The content of most citizen journalism will be familiar to anybody who has ever read a church or community newsletter—it's heartwarming and it probably adds to the store of good things in the world, but it does not mount the collective challenge to power which the traditional media are supposedly too timid to take up. Often the most journalistically impressive material on one of the "hyperlocal" citizen-journalism sites has links to professional journalism, as in the *Northwest Voice,* or *Chi-Town Daily News,* where much of the material is written by students at Northwestern University's Medill School of Journalism, who are in training to take up full-time jobs in news organizations. At the highest level of journalistic achievement, the reporting that revealed the civil-liberties encroachments of the war on terror, which has upset the Bush Administration, has come from old-fashioned big-city newspapers and television networks, not Internet journalists; day by day, most independent accounts of world events have come from the same traditional sources. Even at its best and most ambitious, citizen journalism reads like a decent Op-Ed page, and not one that offers daring, brilliant, forbidden opinions that would otherwise be unavailable. Most citizen journalism reaches very small and specialized audiences and is proudly minor in its concerns. David Weinberger, another advocate of news-media journalism, has summarized the situation with a witty play on Andy Warhol's maxim: "On the Web, everyone will be famous to fifteen people."

There is not much relation between claims for the possibilities inherent in journalist-free journalism and what the people engaged in that pursuit are actually producing.

Reporting—meaning the tradition by which a member of a distinct occupational category gets to cross the usual bounds of geography and class, to go where important things are happening, to ask powerful people blunt and impertinent questions, and to report back, reliably and in plain language, to a general audience—is a distinctive, fairly recent invention. It probably started in the United States, in the mid-nineteenth century, long after the Founders wrote the First Amendment. It has spread—and it continues to spread—around the world.

It is a powerful social tool, because it provides citizens with an independent source of information about the state and other holders of power. It sounds obvious, but reporting requires reporters. They don't have to be priests or gatekeepers or even paid professionals; they just have to go out and do the work.

The Internet is not unfriendly to reporting; potentially, it is the best reporting medium ever invented. A few places, like the site on Yahoo! operated by Kevin Sites, consistently offer good journalism that has a distinctly Internet, rather than re-purposed, feeling. To keep pushing in that direction, though, requires that we hold up original reporting as a virtue and use the Internet to find new ways of presenting fresh material—which, inescapably, will wind up being produced by people who do that full time, not "citizens" with day jobs.

Journalism is not in a period of maximal self-confidence right now, and the Internet's cheerleaders are practically laboratory specimens of maximal self-confidence. They have got the rhetorical upper hand; traditional journalists answering their challenges often sound either clueless or cowed and apologetic. As of now, though, there is not much relation between claims for the possibilities inherent in journalist-free journalism and what the people engaged in that pursuit are actually producing. As journalism moves to the Internet, the main project ought to be moving reporters there, not stripping them away.

Blogging Results in Instant Obsolescence

Trevor Butterworth

Trevor Butterworth is a British writer based in Washington, D.C.

Blogging would have been little more than a recipe for even more Internet tedium if it had not been seized upon in the US as a direct threat to the mainstream media and the conventions by which they control news. And one of the conventions that happened to work in blogging's favour was the way the media take a new trend and describe it as a revolution. The surge of hype about blogging was helped by the fact that many of the most prominent bloggers were high-fliers within the media establishment—such as Andrew Sullivan, a former editor of the *New Republic,* or Mickey Kaus of *Slate,* the online magazine Microsoft sold to the Washington Post Company [in 2005].

That such established journalists were blogging gave the revolution a dose of credibility that it might not have had if it were in the hands of true outsiders. And then, just before the presidential election in 2004, blogging had its Battleship Potemkin moment, when swarms of partisan bloggers rose up to sink CBS's iron-jawed leviathan Dan Rather for peddling supposedly fake memos about [President George W.] Bush's national guard service.

This seemed to prove one of blogging's biggest selling points—that the collective intelligence of the media's audience was greater than the collective intelligence of any news programme or newspaper.

It also showed that blogging was irrepressible—that power was shifting from the gatekeepers of the traditional media to a more open, fluid information society that would have gladdened the heart of the philosopher Karl Popper. And it solidified the belief among conservatives that blogging was a way to take down their longstanding enemies in the once impregnable fortress of the liberal press.

Is Blogging an Information Revolution?

As syndicated radio host and law professor Hugh Hewitt wrote in the conservative *Weekly Standard* last August [2005], "It is hard to overstate the speed with which the information reformation is advancing—or to overestimate its impact on politics and culture. The mainstream media is a hollowed-out shell of its former self when it comes to influence, and when advertisers figure out who is reading the blogs, the old media is going to see their advertising base drain away, and not slowly."

Isn't the problem of the media right now that we barely have time to read a newspaper, let alone traverse the thoughts of a million bloggers?

We are witnessing "the dawn of a blogosphere dominant media", announced Michael S. Malone, who has been described as "the Boswell of Silicon Valley". "Five years from now, the blogosphere will have developed into a powerful economic engine that has all but driven newspapers into oblivion, has morphed (thanks to cell phone cameras) into a video medium that challenges television news and has created a whole new group of major media companies and media superstars. Billions of dollars will be made by those prescient enough to either get on board or invest in these companies."

Even the ne plus ultra [cream] of American public intellectuals, Richard Posner, senior lecturer in law at the University of Chicago, former chief judge on the US Court of Appeals for the Seventh Circuit, declared blogging to be "the latest and perhaps gravest challenge to the journalistic establishment" (although it is worth noting that Judge Posner decided to publish his meditation in the *New York Times Book Review* rather than on his own blog).

But as with any revolution, we must ask whether we are being sold a naked emperor. Is blogging really an information revolution? Is it about to drive the mainstream news media into oblivion? Or is it just another crock of virtual gold—a meretricious equivalent of all those noisy Internet start-ups that were going to build a brave "new economy" a few years ago?

Shouldn't we just be a tiny bit sceptical of another information revolution following on so fast from the last one—especially as this time round no one is even pretending to be getting rich? Isn't the problem of the media right now that we barely have time to read a newspaper, let alone traverse the thoughts of a million bloggers?

The democratic promise of blogs ... has just produced more fragmentation and segregation at a time when seeing the totality of things—the purview of old media—is arguably much more important.

I suspect so, not least because the "dinosaur" businesses of the old economy have a canny ability to absorb, adapt and evolve. We are already starting to see blogs taking root in well established newspapers on both sides of the Atlantic, though few have yet gone as far as the *News & Record* in Greensboro, North Carolina, where, [in 2005], editor John Robinson told his reporters to turn themselves into bloggers. He also invited readers to act as reporters, filing their own stories, and writes a regular blog himself.

Some experiments have gone awry. When the *Los Angeles Times* decided to try letting readers insert their own ideas into its editorials online [in 2005], the trial ended within days after obscene pictures were posted on its site.

Some Blogging Enthusiasts Now Doubt Its Significance

But as the old media wrestle with the significance of blogging, it is sobering to hear some of the heroes of the "revolution" now speak of its insignificance. Late last year [2005], I went to the ramshackle East Village apartment of Choire (pronounced "Corey") Sicha, a former gallery owner and now a senior editor at the *New York Observer*, a vibrant weekly newspaper that covers the rich and powerful of Manhattan.

Dressed in a pink shirt and blue jeans, and unshaven to the point of looking like a young Bee Gee gone preppy, Sicha is less than starry-eyed about blogging—even though it helped put him and [the satirical blog] Gawker on the media map.

"The word blogosphere has no meaning," he said from across a folding table vast enough to support the battle of Waterloo in miniature (the apartment owes much to eBay, the Ikea of bohemia). "There is no sphere; these people aren't connected; they don't have anything to do with each other." The democratic promise of blogs, he explained, has just produced more fragmentation and segregation at a time when seeing the totality of things—the purview of old media—is arguably much more important.

"As for blogs taking over big media in the next five years? Fine, sure," he added. "But where are the beginnings of that? Where is the reporting? Where is the reliability? The rah-rah blogosphere crowd are apparently ready to live in a world without war reporting, without investigative reporting, without nearly any of the things we depend on newspapers for. The world of blogs is like an entire newspaper composed of op-eds and letters and wire service feeds. And they're all excited about the global reach of blogs? Right, tell it to China."

If the hype surrounding blogging sounds familiar, it's only because you really have heard it all before. In Washington DC, the fiery-haired woman behind the Wonkette blog, Ana Marie Cox found the idea of blogging's grave threats and grand promises rife with déjà vu. "People said this about [fan] zines too," she said. "People said this about the Web in general as well—oh God, they probably said this about CD-roms."...

Blogging in the US is not reflective of the kind of deep social and political change that lay behind the alternative press in the 1960s.

If anyone ought to be a true believer in the blogging revolution, it's Cox; but she isn't. "I just don't see the 'lumbering dinosaurs of mainstream media'—there's no asteroid coming," she said. "They may have—to push the metaphor wildly—to learn to live in an ecosphere where there is a more limited amount of whatever it is."

"Food?" I ventured.

"Food," she agreed. "But there's always going to be a *New York Times*. As a culture, we like to have a narrative that we kind of agree on. You and your cohorts may believe that it's liberal elitist propaganda—or you may think it's corporate, conservative hegemony. But there's a sense in which it's good to have the *New York Times* because we need to know that this is the dominant storyline right now. Cable news has the same function. I guess the idea is that in Jakarta somebody at their computer is going to type up a news story about what's going on in Jakarta. But you know, I think I do want a professional reporter doing that as well."

The Weakness of Blogging in the United States

Cox also stands as a prime example of another under-acknowledged weakness of the blogger uprising: to make it in blogging seems to mean making it out of blogging....

And if Gawker was a kind of guilty pleasure people enjoyed after the horror of 9/11 had lingered just a little too long, it is a pleasure that has begun testing readers' limits....

The Gawker spirit is wearing a little thin in light of a seemingly endless bloody insurgency in Iraq, a mesmerising failure of government to deal with the massive catastrophe of Hurricane Katrina, and revelations of corruption on Capitol Hill. "Satire," said Choire Sicha, "is the most useless cultural effluvia one could possibly produce out of the cultural situation in America right now."

In many respects, the American media in all their stuffy isolation brought the bloggers upon themselves. When I first arrived in Washington in 1993, Martin Walker, then bureau chief of the *Guardian*, made the acid and insightful comment that you had to be old to be allowed to have an opinion in print in the US press. In contrast to the British and European media, which had their origins in the Enlightenment and the belief that journalism was a forum for debate and argument—even philosophy, according to David Hume—the American press is a 19th century creation animated by the pursuit of fact.

Blogging—if you will forgive the cartoon philosophising—brought the European Enlightenment to the US. Each blogger was his, or her, own printing press, spontaneously exercising their freedom to criticise. Which is great. But along the way, opinion became the new pornography on the Internet.

The voices with the loudest volume in the blogosphere definitely belong to people who have experience writing.

The historical lesson here is one of cyclical rebellion at the US media for being staid, dull and closed off to change. Indeed, the underground press of the 1960s was described in almost identical terms as blogging is today. "The loudest voice heard in America these days," said the radical journalist Andrew Kopkind in 1967, "is the sound of insurgents chiselling away at establishments."

The present round of chiselling may feel exciting and radically new—but blogging in the US is not reflective of the kind of deep social and political change that lay behind the alternative press in the 1960s. Instead, its dependency on old media for its material brings to mind [eighteenth-century satirist Jonathan] Swift's fleas sucking upon other fleas "ad infinitum": somewhere there has to be a host for feeding to begin. That blogs will one day rule the media world is a triumph of optimism over parasitism.

Blogs Are Needed in Closed Societies

This is patently not the case in other parts of the world. "In a market like the US, blogs are superabundant and often irrelevant because we suffer from a glut of data and have lost our norms for creating information hierarchies," said Anne Nelson, a media consultant and adjunct professor at the Columbia School of International and Public Affairs. "In authoritarian societies like Syria or China, it's the reverse—people lack independent information and may question the imposed hierarchy. In fact, as Nasrin Alavi notes in her recent book, *We Are Iran*, blogging is creating an information revolution where the Iranian regime has been stunningly successful at shutting down newspapers (41 over the past decade)." ...

Blogging will no doubt always have a place as an underground medium in closed societies; but for those in the west trying to blog their way into viable businesses, the economics are daunting. The inherent problem with blogging is that your brand resides in individuals. If they are fabulous writers, someone is likely to lure them away to a better salary and the opportunity for more meaningful work; if the writer tires and burns out, the brand may go down in flames with them. ...

The dismal traffic numbers also point to another little trade secret of the blogosphere, and one missed by Judge Posner and all the other blog-evangelists when they extol the idea that blogging allows thousands of Tom Paines to bloom. As

Ana Marie Cox says: "When people talk about the liberation of the armchair pajamas media, they tend to turn a blind eye to the fact that the voices with the loudest volume in the blogosphere definitely belong to people who have experience writing. They don't have to be experienced journalists necessarily, but they write—part of their professional life is to communicate clearly in written words."

The vast wasteland of verbiage produced by the relentless nature of blogging is the single greatest impediment to its seriousness as a medium.

And not every blogger can be a Tom Paine. "People may want a democratic media," says Cox, "but they don't want to be bored. They also want to be entertained and they want to feel like they've learned something. They want ideas expressed with some measure of clarity."

Which brings us to the spectre haunting the blogosphere—tedium. If the pornography of opinion doesn't leave you longing for an eroticism of fact, the vast wasteland of verbiage produced by the relentless nature of blogging is the single greatest impediment to its seriousness as a medium.

Would Political Writers of the Past Have Blogged?

To illustrate the point, I asked a number of bloggers whether they thought Karl Marx or George Orwell, two enormously potent political writers who were also journalists, would have blogged if the medium had been available to them. And almost always, the answer was, why of course, it would have given them the widest possible audience and the greatest possible impact.

"We're sure Marx and Orwell would have blogged," said Heather and Jessica of gofugyourself.com. "When it comes right down to it, blogs reach the greatest amount of people in the least amount of time, and they reach the very people Marx and Orwell wanted to speak to most."

Any writer of talent needs the time and peace to produce work that has a chance of enduring.

"Orwell, definitely," said Instapundit's Glenn Reynolds. "Marx would have had to acquire a bit more 'snap', I'm afraid, to have made it as a blogger."

"Orwell maybe," said Cox. "Orwell was pathologically productive. He never doubted himself, that's for sure. And maybe he shares that trait with many bloggers."

The question was, of course, rigged. The great critic and editor Cyril Connolly fell into despair over the prolixity of Orwell's wartime writing: "Being Orwell, nothing he wrote is quite without value and unexpected gems keep popping up. But O the boredom of argument without action, politics without power.". . .

The point is, any writer of talent needs the time and peace to produce work that has a chance of enduring. Connolly provided that to Orwell with the influential literary magazine he co-edited, *Horizon*, a publication that gave Orwell the chance to write some of his most memorable essays.

Blogging is the closest literary culture has come to instant obsolescence.

As for Marx, journalism was an act of economic necessity that, initially, necessitated [fellow socialist Friedrich] Engels doing all the writing. But Marx was a quick learner with a deft wit, and in his brisk biography, Francis Wheen posits that "had he but world enough and time Marx could have made his name as the sharpest polemical journalist of the 19th century. But at his back he could always hear the nagging voice of conscience whispering, 'c'est magnifique, mais c'est ne pas la guerre." [Loosely translated, "It's great, but it's not what I'm fighting for."] For Marx and Engels, journalism was trivial—an impediment to serious, memorable and above all influential work. "Mere potboiling," wrote Engels of the more than 500 articles he and Marx wrote for the *New York Daily Tribune*, "It doesn't matter if they are never read again."

And that, in the end, is the dismal fate of blogging: it renders the word even more evanescent than journalism; yoked, as bloggers are, to the unending cycle of news and the need to post four or five times a day, five days a week, 50 weeks of the year, blogging is the closest literary culture has come to instant obsolescence. No Modern Library edition of the great polemicists of the blogosphere to yellow on the shelf; nothing but a virtual tomb for a billion posts—a choric song of the word-weary bloggers, forlorn mariners forever posting on the slumberless seas of news.

CHAPTER 2

Do Blogs Have Significant Impact on American Politics?

Chapter Preface

Within the past few years, blogging has entered the mainstream of politics. As Laura Gordon-Murnane of the Bureau of National Affairs wrote in the October 2006 issue of *Searcher* magazine, "Political activism, in all its messy glory, has come to the Web and bloggers are among its leading champions."

Of course, individual bloggers have always discussed political issues—often heatedly—in their own blogs, and some of these blogs have attracted large audiences. But now the attempt to raise funds and influence voters through blogging is becoming more organized. Candidates for political office, as well as activist groups, are realizing that because the public is turning more and more to blogs rather than to mainstream media for current information, they cannot afford to be without a presence in the blogosphere.

Although there was some organized political blogging in 2004, the 2008 presidential campaign is the first in which it will play a major role. The extent to which it will influence the outcome of the election is not yet known, but there is certainly no lack of interest on the part of bloggers. A recently opened site, Wonkosphere.com, is "designed for all political writers and bloggers, media people in newspaper, TV, and radio, political workers, activists, and political junkies who need to stay on top of the 2008 Presidential race but can't spend all day searching for the hottest and most relevant material." It uses special software to track hundreds of the most important conservative, liberal, and independent blogs and objectively analyze their content, reporting every four hours on each candidate's "buzz share" and the tone of what is being said about that candidate, with summaries of news about him or her. Its FAQ explains, "Wonkosphere enables you to go beyond your Favorites List and track blogs that perhaps are not on your radar screen, without getting sucked into the black hole of reading everything."

Whether a significant number of readers do go beyond their favorite blogs is a question with strong bearing on the overall impact of political blogging. In theory, blogging provides an opportunity for ordinary Americans to participate more fully in democracy than was possible when ideas and opinions flowed only from the media to passive readers or listeners who had no means of interaction with those who presented them. The ideal envisioned by many blog enthusiasts is of an era in which citizens are well informed about the issues in an election, discuss them, and base their votes on personal evaluation of opposing arguments. But is that what blogging really leads to, or are people simply seeking out blogs that reinforce their own existing biases? Though there are popular blogs representing a wide variety of different political perspectives, most readers follow only those written by commentators with whom they already agree—and political blogs tend to be more one-sided and emotionally charged than the mainstream media ever were. So, although blogging may affect the popularity of specific candidates with similar views, it remains to be seen whether it will have any net influence on which party wins the election.

Nevertheless, the availability of unedited blogs gives citizens access to information that was previously unavailable. It is no longer possible for candidates to cover up facts that they would rather the voters did not know. Moreover, bloggers and followers of blogs *believe* that they are actively participating in the political process, and are therefore more likely to take an interest in it than they would have otherwise. This alone will result in a higher level of citizen involvement than existed in the past.

Blogging Is a Major Development in the Future of Politics

Biz Stone

Biz Stone is the cofounder of the social networking service Twitter. He is the author of several books on blogging.

In the hours after the September 11 attacks on the United States, the Web came alive. Anyone who runs a community website or service can show you the record-breaking spike in their server logs on that day and the days that followed. Blogs were no exception. In fact, people were using blogs to let friends and loved ones know they were okay. Bloggers in Manhattan were chronicling the sights and sounds of their city in the wake of these unbelievable events. Web surfers turned to these blogs to find out what was really going on, to be directed via well-chosen links to news stories with new information, to get a sense of perspective from a real person. From this burst of Web activity, political blogging was born.

They were called warbloggers originally, but as time has gone on they evolved into the broader political realm. Since 9/11, the political blogosphere has been an expanding space filled with argument and camaraderie. Traditional journalists are blogging as are bloggers who've never before written for publication. Most of the blogs are labors of love, though some have managed to make money from their blogs through donations and advertising. Beyond the ability to generate revenue, the most heavily trafficked political bloggers have something even more powerful: influence.

Whether they are liberals, conservatives, libertarians, or anarchists, political bloggers all agree on the power of blogging. They are a community of outspoken political junkies who, even when they are disagreeing with other bloggers, still freely share the coin of the blogosphere: hyperlinks, links that users follow to jump from one blog to the next and that promote each blog even more. These bloggers are a strong community of individuals who realize they don't have the same influence as, say, the *New York Times*—yet.

But these political bloggers' power is even more impressive when you realize that they are influencing the influencers. Journalists look to the political blogosphere for fodder, commentary, quotes, and information. Given their track record and increasing readership, reporters must consider the political bloggerati when filing their stories—those facts better be checked or you might just have a Tennessee law professor pointing out your mistakes to his hundred thousand daily readers. Double check.

Who Are Political Bloggers?

Andrew Sullivan is an independent journalist for the *Sunday Times* of London and the former editor of the *New Republic*, a magazine he still writes for. His blog, Andrew Sullivan's Daily Dish, provides news and links to various controversial stories. His site, andrewsullivan.com, gets around sixty thousand visitors a day according to his public site meter.

Glen Reynolds is the web's Instapundit. His commentaries on politics, science, and culture are published daily to the world's most visited single-author blog—his. Visited avidly by about one hundred and twenty thousand people a day, Instapundit has more fans than most city dailies or cable news shows. If you have a modem, Reynolds has an opinion.

Mainstream news media are forced to follow stories bloggers just won't let lie.

Markos Moulitsas Zuniga was born on September 11, 1971. His blog, Daily Kos, was born on May 26, 2002. Zuniga's liberal-leaning political blog receives over 2.5 million unique visits per month and he has turned his success into a venture—his consulting firm that specializes in the use of emergent technologies in political campaigns.

These men are the political protobloggers. They are the bloggers who spawn *blogchildren*—people who have been inspired to start a blog by reading someone else's. So not only do these popular political blogs enjoy vast numbers of readers, they also spawn more bloggers in their likeness who also grow an audience. In this way, the political blogosphere continues to expand and gain influence.

Blog for America: A Bubble of Community

Blog for America was the official blog of the Howard Dean for America presidential campaign. It started on March 15, 2003, and is considered the first-ever official blog of a presidential candidate. Dean's blog was updated and maintained by staff and guest writers as well as other contributors, but the real magic was in the comments feature.

On average, Dean's blog received about two thousand three hundred comments per day, and the campaign crew read all of them. When ideas, slogans, activities, and events were put into action from people's comments on the blog, Dean supporters knew that they had a very real part in the campaign. The blog had an infectious feeling of optimism; Dean supporters could join in on the campaign no matter where they were.

The Blog for America gave life to "deanspace"—a centralized bubble of support for the campaign. Dean's blog invented him. It put him on the map. In a world where journalists and reporters ask Google for their sound bites, Dean's blog and its supporters had them ready in the form of posts and comments. The blog was both a virtual meeting space and a machine for generating buzz and excitement.

That buzz and excitement might have hurt Dean at the same time it helped. The bubble of passion that grew around the blog was just that—a bubble. It's important to remember that while a blog is a strong tool for building a virtual community, it's still virtual. It's like when you run three miles a day on a treadmill all winter and on the first beautiful spring day you factor in that same half hour for a nice, outdoor jog—but it takes you an hour. There are hills, stoplights, curbs, and people in your way. It's the real world, and you're not in as good shape as you thought you were.

Deanspace was filled with Dean supporters. They whipped one another up into a frenzy. They lived in an echo chamber. Traditional media were attracted to this hub of online activity, and from that perspective it looked like Dean was way out in front, until the actual campaigning began and he started running into some of those hills and stoplights. It's key to remember that a blog and the community that surrounds it can open doors, but you can't rely on it entirely—unless you're running for virtual president.

Democratic Journalism

Dean kicked it off, and within months the blogging of the president 2004 was a given for the other campaigns. John Edwards, Wesley Clarke, Joe Lieberman, George Bush, and John Kerry all started rounding up their supporters on the Web with presidential campaign blogs. If they didn't own some of the intellectual space in the blogosphere, the political bloggers would own it all and would have to speak for them on the Web. In 2004, bloggers were credentialed at the Democratic and Republican conventions.

In the 2004 presidential election, the boys on the bus were joined by the political bloggers. Standing on their software soapboxes, these laptop pundits planted the seeds of change. Their mission was to influence political journalism and maybe even democracy as we know it by taking control of the Internet and beaming their ideas into the minds of millions before big media had time to let the ink dry.

Unrestricted, unedited websites powered by passionate individuals can command the readership of a city daily and break important news gathered from e-mail tips and personal networks of sources. They're not all professionals; there's no editing going on; and usually there's not even a hint of objectivity. Still, these bloggers are reshaping political journalism and building a new force to be reckoned with.

Mainstream news media are forced to follow stories bloggers just won't let lie, like the scandal that ousted Senate Majority Leader Trent Lott, which Glen Reynolds and Josh Marshall refused to let die. Bloggers are a major development in the future of politics, taking the media out of corporate hands and giving them to the people. Two thousand four will be remembered as the year the Internet became a necessity for campaigning.

Blogs Are a Critical Part of Political Commentary

Carla Marinucci

Carla Marinucci is a political reporter for the San Francisco Chronicle.

When Democrats gathered at their candidate-rich California state convention five years ago [2001], a lone blogger from Berkeley was the first, and only, one of his kind to apply for media credentials to cover the events.

Today, an army has arrived in the wake of Markos Moulitsas Zúniga, founder of Daily Kos—one of the nation's most highly trafficked Web logs, which boasts about 600,000 daily readers.

This year [2007], a record 50 Internet-publication bloggers will join the estimated 400 credentialed "mainstream" media in the press room to track the doings of seven Democratic presidential candidates and 2,100 California party delegates.

And those numbers don't count the estimated dozens of mainstream media journalists who will be blogging for major newspapers or the unknown numbers of delegates who will be producing their own running commentary of the convention.

Political parties and candidates understand that bloggers have become a critical part of the commentary on political developments.

"What this is doing is blowing apart the old calculus for who gets to come to the party and who doesn't," says Peter

Leyden, director of the San Francisco–based New Politics Institute, a think tank that tracks the intersection of the Internet and politics.

Blogs Will Influence the 2008 Election

With the 2008 presidential election just 556 days away, political parties and candidates understand that bloggers have become a critical part of the commentary on political developments "on a scale that is absolutely astounding," he said.

"Many of them have passionate followers, people who are crazy about politics," Leyden said. "And if you legitimize them, and bring them into inner circles . . . they will get a huge new segment of folks energized that aren't necessarily reading newspapers and aren't involved in politics."

Experts say the increased presence of bloggers at such traditional events will be closely watched to track their growing influence and analyze how their coverage shapes the candidates' strategies in the 2008 presidential election.

Bob Brigham, 29, an Internet strategist and blogger for Calitics, a liberal Web site that provides commentary on Democratic politics, said the intensity of the "netroots" coverage "stretches the debate in terms of breadth and depth" and has the potential to create immediate ripple effects among a hardcore dedicated political audience.

"If someone has a breakaway speech like (Howard) Dean had four years ago, it could be a paradigm shift in the conventional wisdom about the race," said Brigham, who produces regular commentary on Calitics under his "blogswarm" sign-on. "And if someone gets booed this year, it won't be an item in a sixth paragraph of a news story—it will be on the front page on all of the blogs."

Such efforts are gaining more recognition.

Frank Russo, 55, who became the first blogger and "new media" journalist to get a state press credential, said that increasingly, bloggers try to "bring some coverage and some light to matters that would not otherwise be covered by the mainstream press."

Russo, the former legal counsel to Willie Brown when Brown was Assembly speaker, founded the California Progress Report [in 2006] to provide Democrats with a daily briefing on politics and policy in the state Capitol.

Blog readers and writers say they welcome the increased sunshine on political goings-on.

Bloggers ... often write under anonymous sign-ons and without the bureaucracy or controls of a mainstream media organization.

"The Democratic Party shouldn't be a secret club," said Gloria Nieto, the former chair of the Democratic National Committee's gay and lesbian caucus—and a blogger. "This makes it accessible to a much broader group."

Role of Blogs and Mainstream Media Are Different

The bloggers acknowledge that their role in reporting is vastly different from that of the mainstream reporters sitting next to them in the press room. Many bloggers are openly and passionately partisan about the Democratic cause, and they will cover the caucus meetings, speeches and resolutions with the kind of intensity that appeals to the activist but often not the general reading audience.

While mainstream reporters must sign their names to news stories and submit to the editors and ethical guidelines of their organizations, the bloggers—many operating freelance—often write under anonymous sign-ons and without the bureaucracy or controls of a mainstream media organization.

Brian Leubitz, 28, a UC [University of California] Berkeley master's candidate in public policy—and the founder and editor of Calitics—said he'll attend the convention with nine staffers, the youngest 18 years old, a team larger than many major newspapers will send.

Leubitz said he's seen the growing hunger for blogger perspective since he started his Web log in 2005 to vent his outrage after Hurricane Katrina, when his handful of readers included "my mother." Today, he has 5,000 readers daily who tune in for entertaining, informative and occasionally caustic offerings that range from strategy to gossip.

Both the rewards—and negative impacts—of such coverage have yet to be fully calculated, experts said.

Blogger coverage at a state political convention has the potential to reach "hundreds of thousands of Democrats in our party, and we are so much more because of it," said Eric Jaye, a Democratic strategist who is advising Charlie Brown, a Democratic House candidate who challenged Republican Rep. John Doolittle of Rocklin (Placer County) last fall [2006] and will do so again in 2008.

"It has put races in play that would not have been in play and taken huge parts of America that were no-go zones, and it's turning them from red to blue," Jaye said of the Internet activity among activists. "Thanks to the blogosphere, we're becoming a national party again—not just a party of two coasts."

Blogs Can Have Negative Effects

But one key state Democratic strategist, speaking on the condition of anonymity because of concern for riling the netroots crowd, warns that such efforts are potentially positive and negative.

Netroots commentary can frequently be intensely personal, even "totally mean and irrational," the strategist said, with some bloggers finding power in their ability "to assassinate political characters online."

"It's amplified by the anonymity, and it can be scary that it's so irresponsible," the insider said. "And it's pulling the mainstream media in that direction."

Leyden said in the brave, new and often anarchical world of netroots, there has been growing dialogue about standards and ethics among those blogging on the political scene.

As their coverage evolves, the marketplace will determine who succeeds—and which of the estimated 70 million blogs on the Internet today evaporate for lack of interest or readers.

In the meantime, he said, the blogosphere has created its own arena for battle, and "they aren't sitting there watching the gladiators go at it."

The Future Will Not Be Unblogged

David D. Perlmutter

David D. Perlmutter is a senior fellow at Louisiana State University's Reilly Center for Media & Public Affairs and an associate professor of mass communication on the Baton Rouge campus. He edits a political analysis blog.

Like many political junkies, I get my news and opinion fixes from newspapers, television, and specialty newsletters. But I also rely increasingly on blogs, the Web pages that contain both interactive, hyperlinked reportage and commentary. Such information sources are no longer curiosities. For example, Daily Kos (http://www.dailykos.com)—started by Markos Moulitsas Zúniga, who served in the U.S. Army before going to college and law school—includes contributions from a giant group of leftist, liberal, and Democratic bloggers. The Nielsen/NetRatings service reported that in the single month of July 2005, Kos attracted 4.8 million separate visitors. The Kos audience is thus greater than the combined populations of Iowa, where the first presidential caucus takes place, and New Hampshire, site of the first primary, according to the current Democratic party schedule.

It is no surprise, then, that political scientists and scholars of communication from many disciplines are asking what role blogs will play in future campaigns and elections and, more specifically, how bloggers will affect the election of our next commander in chief.

Media attention to blogging has exploded, in part because of a number of what I call blogthroughs, events that allowed bloggers to demonstrate their powers of instant response, cumulative knowledge, and relentless drumbeating. Those incidents included bloggers' role in challenging the memo about President Bush's National Guard service revealed on CBS, which may have led to Dan Rather's resignation as anchor of the network's evening news; video logs of the tsunami in Southeast Asia; and the high-profile use of blogs by Howard Dean's campaign for the last Democratic presidential nomination. Now, according to various measurement and rating services such as Technorati and BlogPulse, tens of millions of Americans are blogging on all kinds of subjects, like diets, relatives, pets, sports, and sex. Bloggers include journalists, marines in Afghanistan, suburban teenagers, law-school professors, senators, and district attorneys.

Of greatest interest to modern students of politics are the blogs that focus on public affairs. Mainstream political news media regularly check what blogs are saying about a given story—or how they created it. Surveys by the Pew Internet & American Life Project and other organizations have found that most contributors to those blogs follow campaigns and political debates and are extremely likely to vote in elections. Politicians and activists are naturally eager to get their message to such a target audience while also bypassing the mainstream media's editorializing and heavy fees for advertising. Yet, as one political consultant I know put it, "The $200-million questions are: What are blogs? How can we use them? What exactly are they good for?"

Even experts cannot answer those questions because political blogs are in a state of flux. Are they a revolution or an evolution in political speech and activism—or a return to the more partisan press of the nation's early days? Will political bloggers challenge or complement traditional politics, political work, and politicians? Are bloggers representative of other Americans, or are they a minority of politically active citizens? How much impact will blogs have on political discourse and, ultimately, on voting behavior? Are they further Balkanizing American politics, with liberals reading only leftist blogs and conservatives reading only rightist ones?

Probably the most important area for research on blogs today is what role they will have in the presidential election of 2008. A necessary starting point is to consider how similar blogs are, as a new medium or genre or venue, to traditional components of presidential politics.

Are Blogs the New Iowa Caucus?

Since the 1970s, candidates who have done well in the presidential-nomination race have appeared early, during what the journalist Arthur Hadley called the "invisible primary." Raising money nationwide, they spend much of it—and much time—in Iowa and New Hampshire.

Does blog activism go beyond cyberspace and lead to election victory?

But if we think of "blogland" as a place, it is the real "first in the nation" testing ground: Bloggers generally decide whom to support for president (and whom to vociferously oppose) long before states hold caucuses and primaries. Furthermore, like the residents of the small towns in Iowa and New Hampshire, who have long been accustomed to individual attention from campaigners, bloggers cannot be swayed by one-size-fits-all pitches. The essence of blogging, after all, is personal connections between participants—the ability to talk and to talk back, the interplay of argument and critique. John Edwards, former senator and [2004] vice-presidential nominee [who was a candidate in the 2008 presidential primaries but dropped out, pursued] . . . such a strategy: Not only does he have his own blog . . . and post on others' blogs, but at live speaking engagements, he often invites local bloggers to a face-to-face meeting and briefing.

But the big issue for deciding whether bloggers are like early caucus or primary voters is, to paraphrase the advertising slogan for Las Vegas, "Does what starts on the Web stay on the Web?" In other words, does blog activism go beyond cyberspace and lead to election victory?

In 2003, for example, Howard Dean's campaign motivated hundreds of thousands of Americans via blogs and the Internet. His list of registered supporters online grew to 600,000. (A Dean worker lamented to me, "If only we could get them to move to New Hampshire!") He seemed to have entered a new world of horizontal democracy, upsetting the old-boy, rich-man politics with events like an online fund-raising "dinner," during which he ate a turkey sandwich while offering comments about the issues of the day and the campaign.

However, when bloggers take to the streets on behalf of their candidates, they may not be as convincing as old-fashioned political workers. More than 100,000 Dean supporters, many of them motivated young people from exotic places like Seattle and New York, flooded Iowa before the caucuses. I did not meet any there who had pierced noses or spiked hair, but young, eager folks from the coasts were not the best people to evangelize middle-class Midwesterners, even those who might agree with Dean on some issues.

Woe to the candidate whose supposedly first-person blog is outed as a prepackaged set of talking points, created by committee.

Basically, the Dean campaign ignored a key political rule: You deploy supporters in their own areas. People are more apt to be convinced by people who seem like them. Dean online activism did translate into political participation of the old style, in the activists' own states: According to a study by the

Pew Research Center for the People and the Press, most online partisans of Dean voted in the November presidential election.

Are Blogs Fund-Raising Machines?

Historically, early success in raising money has been essential to winning a major party's presidential nomination. The Dean campaign used the Internet to get millions of people to raise small amounts of money, although Dean attracted few large donors. Before the Iowa caucus, Dean had raised at least $20 million. (Sen. John F. Kerry eventually raised about $80 million online.) On the other hand, as Dean learned, expenses like staff salaries, transportation, get-out-the-vote efforts, and—above all—television ads quickly soak up money; his campaign's coffers were emptied within weeks.

A fund-raising strategy focusing on blogs and other online sources, however, is not always doomed to failure. Most political observers would agree that Dean lost in Iowa and New Hampshire for reasons other than cash flow. Had he been victorious in those early states, his campaign would have attracted many traditional donations, for in politics, money follows the smell of victory.

Are Blog Posts Campaign Literature?

Modern presidential candidates write books, make speeches, participate in debates, and hold press conferences. But their books are little read, even by loyal followers, and their other writings and discourses are mainly vehicles to deliver the seven-second sound bite that their media consultants hope will be picked up by television news.

Furthermore, most of the material that candidates present, from speeches to debate points and even personal letters, is concocted by professional speechwriters, consultants, and members of the campaign staff. Such in-house plagiarism is not considered unethical; every candidate does it. There is some cynicism about this process, but not even the most antagonistic and aggressive reporter will demand of a candidate: "Weren't those remarks written by your speechwriter? How dare you pretend the words are yours?"

Blogs have a different sort of audience. Blog readers go through entire posts carefully, especially those of politicians; they don't just glance at the main headings. And readers demand authenticity. Woe to the candidate whose supposedly first-person blog is outed as a prepackaged set of talking points, created by committee. In short, bloggers—including the people who create the blogs, the people who post on them, and the people who read them regularly—are less an audience or a readership than a community of debaters. It follows that they probably don't want any part of their interaction with a candidate to be (or even to seem) programmed. A further challenge is time: Editing a blog, creating new material day after day, or even hour after hour to keep up with breaking news, is a considerable commitment.

Bloggers tend to be passionate, idealistic about their politics, and unforgiving of the gamesmanship, opinion flopping, yielding to expediency, and compromise that are part of normal politics.

Are Blogs "Meet the Candidate" Get-Togethers?

Politicians have private briefings, talks, and discussions with staff members, party leaders, donors, friends, relatives, and even sympathetic journalists. Blog posts can mimic such intimate encounters for a broader group. However, making public your stream-of-consciousness thoughts on issues of the day, your favorite restaurants, the proper role of parents, and so forth can give your enemies a lot of free ammunition. An old political rule is that the more you say, the more evidence there is with which to hang you.

Obviously candidates and their staffs have worried about that problem, and the result has often been dull blogs, with just as many layers of editing and focus-group testing for entries as for the average speech. Yet the more controlled or canned a blog sounds, the less it feels like a blog.

Are Bloggers Political Operatives?

In the 2004 South Dakota race for U.S. Senate between Democrat Tom Daschle and Republican John Thune, two prominent local bloggers who had attacked the incumbent Democrat turned out to have been given money by the Thune campaign. The payments to the pair were not revealed until after the election, when campaign-finance documents were filed. The effect of such hit-blogs cannot be easily measured, but South Dakota is a lightly populated state, and Thune won by only about 4,500 votes.

So yes, campaigns can use bloggers as paid operatives or subsidized supporters. But the sheer number of political bloggers suggests that it would be very hard to buy up even a small part of blogland that way. Indeed, subsidies are the subject of much mirth among bloggers. The editor of Righting Wisconsin jokes with his readers—that is, I think he is joking—"If you want me to keep my mouth shut, it's gonna cost you some dough. I figure a thousand bucks is reasonable, so I want two" (a quote from the movie *Miller's Crossing*).

You can't pack cyberspace with your supporters, shut out all hecklers, and enforce message discipline.

Furthermore, although bloggers can be a loyal constituency, they are not an unswerving one. When Sen. Richard J. Durbin, a Democrat of Illinois, publicly compared the treatment of prisoners in Guantanamo Bay, Cuba, with that meted out by the Nazis, left-wing bloggers rallied to his defense. He even met with a group of them to get advice. Yet, when he decided to take the politician's customary recourse of apologizing for the remarks, some of those bloggers turned on him, condemning him as a sellout and a fraud.

Are Blogs Campaign Rallies?

Bloggers tend to be passionate, idealistic about their politics, and unforgiving of the gamesmanship, opinion flopping, yielding to expediency, and compromise that are part of normal politics.

In February [2006] Sen. Hillary Rodham Clinton, the former first lady, had the largest war chest, the greatest name recognition, and the highest national-poll ratings of any Democrat expected to run for president in 2008. She is, however, faring poorly on leftist blogs because she has consistently tried to steer a middle course in her policies, presumably to win swing voters. Of course, politicians have always needed to balance between their party's base and the middle of the electorate. But blogs make this tension if not more complicated, at least more public. You can't pack cyberspace with your supporters, shut out all hecklers, and enforce message discipline.

Are Blogs Television Ads?

The 30-second candidate is alive and well; television and the enormous cost of advertising on it will be part of any presidential campaign for the foreseeable future. But blogs offer advantages over the tube. Ads and videos on blogs are not (yet) covered by campaign-reform rules. Blogs and vlogs can test-market a TV video but can also provide an instant response to opponents' attacks without the usual delays of regular media.

Of course, if bloggers don't like a candidate's TV messages, they will say so. Dean bloggers, for instance, expressed their exasperation online when that campaign sputtered. And the bloggers' criticism can easily become fodder for negative coverage in the traditional media.

Comparing political blogs to political television is especially interesting because blogs are arguably part of the evolution of television from a mass to a niche medium. I tell students that successful mass communication is that which best approximates successful interpersonal communication. Great communicators are able to deliver personal and empathetic messages to large audiences.

Blogs . . . may not be as good at changing people's minds as they are at focusing attention on an issue and rallying support.

In my studies of blogging, I have found that the personal factor is also key for bloggers who build loyal audiences. My students, for instance, report that they prefer blogs whose editors they most like, respect, and trust. That relationship is built not on a single post but gradually, over time.

Are Blogs Talk Radio?

Many political insiders would say yes. Bloggers can be attack dogs of the right or left, harping on an issue until it reaches prominence, raising ire in their audience. But they can also provide more reasoned debates. When Sen. Barack Obama, an Illinois Democrat [who as of March 2008 is running for President], posted on various sites—including Daily Kos—a long defense of Democrats who had voted to confirm John G. Roberts Jr. as chief justice (even though Obama himself had voted against confirmation), it was the talk of liberal cyberspace for weeks, the subject of tens of thousands of posts, comments, and debates.

But are bloggers like the host of a talk-radio show, the people who call in, or the listening audience? The term "blogger" is often employed to mean a blog's owner, as well as other posters to the blog and its regular readers. Are those groups the same, though, demographically or psychologically?

Do they have, for example, similar levels of commitment to a political position or an issue? That is a compelling question because research on voting behavior has shown that the higher the level of commitment you have to an idea, cause, issue, or candidate, the less likely you are to be swayed by arguments from the other side. Blogs then may not be as good at changing people's minds as they are at focusing attention on an issue and rallying support.

So far, only a few of the two dozen or so [people who as of 2006 were thought to be] probable and possible Democratic candidates for president in 2008 have their own blogs or contribute regularly to others' blogs: Sen. Evan Bayh, of Indiana; Wesley Clark, the retired general who ran for president in 2004; Hillary Clinton; John Edwards; Sen. Russ Feingold, of Wisconsin; Barack Obama; and Gov. Tom Vilsack, of Iowa. Blogging Republicans who may become candidates include Sen. Bill Frist, of Tennessee, and Newt Gingrich, former speaker of the House.

For all their potential minefields, blogs may be a much safer place for a politician than elected office.

It is interesting how thin the blogs of the would-be presidents are in quantity and quality. Edwards, a prolific blogger and flesh-presser of other bloggers, is almost the only potential candidate to fully dive into the medium. That may be partly because, as was the case with Howard Dean in 2003, he has no place else to go: No longer in the Senate himself, he is not as much in the public eye as many of his likely opponents. His nascent campaign may be a good test case of what blog outreach can do for a candidate.

Of course, for all their potential minefields, blogs may be a much safer place for a politician than elected office. Members of Congress are faced with voting on contentious issues like appropriations for the war in Iraq; often, whatever they do earns them enemies. Edwards can now portray himself as a populist outsider—a role he plainly relishes.

One can imagine why other candidates would avoid blogs. For example, should a front-runner with much to lose risk blogging? Hillary Clinton has participated in the American Cancer Society's Blog for Hope, but her comments are very safely worded and read more like press releases than real posts. Would it make more sense for her to post a blog entry that might not get any big-media attention, or to give a $2,000-a-plate speech that will be picked up by network television? Besides the money, an added appeal to the speech is that her staff can control the crowd to a great extent, guaranteeing a friendly response; that is not possible on blogs.

The instant interaction that blogs encourage can be hazardous for a politician. As a case in point, Wesley Clark's lively group blog (http://www.securingamerica.com) features posts by him and those who register for the site. A live chat with Clark in December [2005] allowed participants to ask him questions on many topics, including the Iraq war, blogging, government wiretapping, U.S. relations with Serbia . . . and UFO's. The general responded to one lengthy post about space aliens with the terse comment that he had "never been briefed" on their supposed landing in Roswell, N.M.

One thing is certain . . . although the future is unknown, it will not be unblogged.

Clark gave direct, if careful, answers to some questions. But sometimes he did not reply at all, presumably because the queries were coming too fast, were too complicated for a quick response, were too politically dangerous to take a position on, or were posted by someone obviously trying to pull his leg. Would any candidate be able to respond at length and in depth without producing inaccuracies and gaffes that would delight his or her opponents? Are the benefits of blogging worth the risks and efforts?

Ours is an exciting era for students of politics and an unnerving time for political professionals, whose tried-and-true strategies are coming under increasing challenge with evolving technology. Clearly blogs are both similar to and unlike many other types of political media. Nevertheless, at this point, any pronouncements about the power of blogs and the potential directions of political blogging would be as foolish as similar prognostications about the trajectory of television news in 1952. One thing is certain: Blogging is now part of political campaigns, elections, and public-affairs debates; although the future is unknown, it will not be unblogged.

Blogs Lack the Depth of Print Journalism

George Packer

George Packer is a staff writer for the New Yorker *and a colum-nist for* Mother Jones *magazine. His articles have appeared in many other major publications, and he is the author of several books.*

First, a confession: I hate blogs. I'm also addicted to them. Hours dissolve into nothing when I suit up and demateri-alize into the political blogosphere, first visiting one of the larger, nearer online opinion diaries—talkingpointsmemo .com, andrewsullivan.com, kausfiles.com—then beaming my-self outward along rays of pixelated light to dozens of satel-lites and lesser stars, Calpundit, InstaPundit, OxBlog, each one radiant with links to other galaxies—online newspapers and magazines with deep, deep archives, think-tank websites, hundred-page electronic reports in PDF—until I'm light-years from the point of departure and can rescue myself only by summoning the will to disconnect from the whole artificial universe. With a jolt, I land in front of my computer. Before long I'll venture forth again to see what's new out there—because the blogosphere changes from instant to instant.

My private habit (and others') has emerged as the journal-istic signature of the 2004 campaign. Although only 13 per-cent of Americans regularly get their campaign news from the Internet—still far less than from local, cable, and network TV news—nonetheless a whole industry of analysts has risen up to declare 2004 the dawn of a new political era. Part of the mystique of blogs is their protean quality: They work both sides of the divide between politics and media, further blurring the already fuzzy distinctions between reporter, pundit, political operative, activist, and citizen. The universe of blogs includes those of both major parties; candidates' campaign websites (most famously, Howard Dean's, which became the hottest organizing tool since direct mail—until it turned into an online echo chamber that failed to deliver actual votes), the blogs of more traditional journalists on the websites of news organizations such as the *New York Times*, the *New Republic*, and ABC; and the proliferation of one-man electronic soap-boxing by the known and the obscure alike.

Bloggers are almost unfailingly contemptuous toward everyone except one another.

Large Claims for Blogs

In other words, the blog documents, comments, and participates. Nothing new here: Theodore H. White grew so close to John F. Kennedy that he ended up writing campaign speeches for the Democratic nominee even as he reported *The Making of the President 1960*. Somewhere out there in the infinite spaces of the Internet floats a site called bloggingofthepresi dent.com, whose homepage declares: "The Blogging of the President (or BOP) is dedicated to the great writer Theodore H. White, whose documentary series of books, *The Making of the President*, inspired generations of journalists. . . . We believe that the story of how America chooses its leader is fundamental to how America conceives of itself, and something about this story changed in 2004. Somehow, HTML and 'blogs' are now pillars of the republic; indeed, a whole new way of doing politics seems emergent and potentially dominant."

BOP then quotes the proclamation, originally made in *Wired*, of Stanford law professor Lawrence Lessig: "When they write the account of the 2004 campaign, it will include at least one word that has never appeared in any presidential history:

blog. Whether or not it elects the next president, the blog may be the first innovation from the Internet to make a real difference in election politics."

These are large claims—and the thought that the republic is perched atop "Kicking Ass: Daily Dispatches From the DNC," let alone such pillars of salt as wonkette.com, frankly makes me nervous. Yet I have to face the fact that blogs are emergent, potentially dominant, and making a real difference in my election year. For a political junkie, they're pure and uncut. If blogs are to our age what White's campaign books were to the dramatic years 1960 to 1972, how is the story changing in 2004?

Far More Is Written than Needs to Be Said

The constellation of opinion called the blogosphere consists, like the stars themselves, partly of gases. This is what makes blogs addictive—that is, both pleasurable and destructive: They're so easy to consume, and so endlessly available. Their second-by-second proliferation means that far more is written than needs to be said about any one thing. To change metaphors for a moment (and to deepen the shame), I gorge myself on these hundreds of pieces of commentary like so much candy into a bloated—yet nervous, sugar-jangled—stupor. Those hours of out-of-body drift leave me with few, if any, tangible thoughts. Blog prose is written in headline form to imitate informal speech, with short emphatic sentences and frequent use of boldface and italics. The entries, sometimes updated hourly, are little spasms of assertion, usually too brief for an argument ever to stand a chance of developing layers of meaning or ramifying into qualification and complication. There's a constant sense that someone (almost always the blogger) is winning and someone else is losing. Everything that happens in the blogosphere—every point, rebuttal, gloat, jeer, or "fisk" (dismemberment of a piece of text with close analytical reading)—is a knockout punch. A curious thing about this rarefied world is that bloggers are almost unfailingly contemptuous toward everyone except one another. They are also nearly without exception men (this form of combat seems too naked for more than a very few women). I imagine them in neat blue shirts, the glow from the screen reflected in their glasses as they sit up at 3:48 a.m. triumphantly tapping out their third rejoinder to the WaPo's press commentary on Tim Russert's on-air recap of the Wisconsin primary.

All of this meta-comment by very bright young men who never leave their rooms is the latest, somewhat debased, manifestation of the old art of political pamphleteering, a lost form in this country through much of the 20th century. The modern American idea of journalism as objectivity, with news and editorial pages strictly separated, emerged in the Progressive Era with books like Walter Lippmann's classic *Public Opinion*. For most of the last century, this idea anointed political journalists as a mandarin class of insiders with serious responsibilities; access was everything. At some point during the Reagan years [1981–1989], this mandarinate lost interest in politics as a contest of beliefs and policies with some bearing on the experience of people unlike themselves. Instead, elite Washington reporters turned their coverage into an account of a closed system, an intricate process, in which perceptions were the only real things and the journalists themselves were intimately involved. The machinations of Michael Deaver and Roger Ailes, followed by Lee Atwater and James Carville, became the central drama. We've grown so familiar with this approach that today you can open the *New York Times* and be unsurprised to find its chief political correspondent, Adam Nagourney, writing about polls and campaign strategies day after day.

Blogs came along to feed off this fascination with the interior mechanics of politics. Many bloggers emerged from the ranks of the press itself; unlike the elite press corps, though, anyone with a computer and an Internet connection can blog.

This is potentially the most radical innovation of the form: It opens up political journalism to a vast marketplace of competitors, reminiscent of earlier ages of pamphleteering. It also restores unvarnished opinion, for better and worse, to a central place in political writing. Insult and invective were the stock-in-trade of the English political essayists of the 18th century, and of their American counterparts during the early years of the republic (when bimbo eruptions made their first appearance in press coverage of presidential campaigns). The explosion of blogs has blown a needed hole in the sealed rooms of the major editorial pages and the Sunday talk shows. It has also affected political reporting, by forcing Washington journalists accustomed to the caution of the mainstream to follow less traveled tributaries—for example, the examination of President Bush's National Guard service was partly pushed along by evidence laid out for reporters by Calpundit.

Blogs Failed to Portray the 2004 Election

And yet, if blogs are "a new way of doing politics," there is also something peculiarly stale and tired about them—not the form, but the content. The campaign of 2004 is important not just for the arrival of blogs. Thanks to September 11, this happens to be one of those rare years when a real election will take place. By "real," I mean an election in which the stakes are genuinely high, the differences between the candidates far-reaching, the consequences for the country and the world potentially huge. 1932 was a real election year; so were 1968 and 1980. We haven't had one since Reagan trounced Carter. Especially during the Clinton years, with the Cold War over and the economy flush, politics grew more and more into a spectacle of personalities and gossip-mongering, a trend both reflected and furthered by the political journalism of those years. Until recently, Frank Rich, a former drama critic, wrote an op-ed column for the *Times* largely devoted to reviewing politics as entertainment.

Campaign coverage in 2004 still belongs to that era—nowhere more than in the blogosphere, where the claustrophobic effect of the echo chamber and the hall of mirrors is at its most intense, where the reverberations of trivialities last far longer than in print or on TV. This new pillar of the republic turns out to be an inadequate mode for capturing a real election.

Rather than imitating or reproducing external reality, [the blogosphere] exists alongside, detached, self-encased, in a stance of ironic or combative appraisal.

So far this year [2004], bloggers have been remarkably unadept at predicting events (as have reporters, who occupy a different part of the same habitat). Most of them failed to foresee Dean's rise, Dean's fall, Kerry's resurgence, Bush's slippage. Above all, they didn't grasp the intensity of feeling among Democratic primary voters—the resentments still glowing hot from Florida 2000, the overwhelming interest in economic and domestic issues, the personal antipathy toward Bush, the resurgence of activism, the longing for a win. The blogosphere was often caught surprised by these passions and the electoral turns they caused. Rather than imitating or reproducing external reality, it exists alongside, detached, self-encased, in a stance of ironic or combative appraisal. Theodore H. White's books, as well as the magazine form of nonfiction narrative known as New Journalism that was as characteristic of the '60s as blogs are of this decade, gave readers the sense—illusory, of course—that they were watching a coherent story unfold from a front row (or even backstage) seat. *The Making of the President* turned politics into the stuff of high novelistic drama, with larger-than-life acute ideological conflict played out in halls of power and city streets. The style of thickly descriptive storytelling, based on heavy reporting, immersed readers in the arc of an election year, achieving a sense of unity between the protagonists and the spectators, so that the campaign seemed to involve the whole of American society in the theatrics.

Blogging Is Detached from the Real World

Blogs, by contrast, are atomized, fragmentary, and of the instant. They lack the continuity, reach, and depth to turn an election into a story. When one of the best of the bloggers, Joshua Micah Marshall of talkingpointsmemo.com, brought his laptop to New Hampshire and tried to cover the race in the more traditional manner, the results were less than satisfying; his posts failed to convey the atmosphere of those remarkable days between Iowa and the first primary. Marshall couldn't turn his gift for parsing the news of the moment to the more patient task of turning reportage into scenes and characters so that the candidates and the voters take life online. He didn't function as a reporter; there was, as there often is with blogs, too much description of where he was sitting, what he was thinking, who'd just walked into the room, as if the enclosed space in which bloggers carry out their work had followed Marshall to New Hampshire and kept him encased in its bubble. He might as well have been writing from his apartment in Washington. But the failure wasn't personal; this particular branch of the Fourth Estate just doesn't lend itself to sustained narrative and analysis. Blogs remain private, written in the language and tone of knowingness, insider shorthand, instant mastery. Read them enough and any subject will go dead.

I went to New Hampshire the weekend before the primary because, for all the millions of words written in both blogs and conventional journalism, I suspected that I'd been missing something. It was true: I felt at once that something more interesting than the usual quadrennial spectacle was going on. There were large crowds everywhere, with a strong current of excitement—not just because the horse race was then wide

open, but because its outcome so obviously matters. The issues, not the personalities, filled those rooms. In 2004 the
public seems to have rediscovered politics. But I had to go to
New Hampshire to find out. I blame my addiction.

Specific Blogs Reach Only Small Segments of the Population

Byron York

Byron York is a White House correspondent for National Review *magazine. He has written for many other major national publications and is a frequent guest on television and radio.*

While there is no universally accepted standard of measurement for the readership of blogs [influential left-wing bloggers Markos] Moulitsas and [Jerome] Armstrong claim that the top 70 liberal blogs attract about 60 million "page views" per month. It's not clear how many people that means, although Moulitsas claims his blog reaches about 1 million people per week. But even if the real figure is significantly lower, and many observers think it is, there is no doubt that Daily Kos, like the left-wing blogosphere general, has lots of readers.

Of course, so do blogs on the right. The difference is that bloggers on the right spend most of their time commenting on the news of the day, while bloggers on the left claim to be building a new political movement, one that is revolutionizing Democratic-party politics. Listen to liberal bloggers talk and it won't be long before they say they are "building communities." "Progressive blogs build communities of activists and generate new political activity online," says a key study of the blogosphere, done for the Washington-based New Democrat Network, an early booster of Moulitsas [and] Armstrong. "The progressive blogosphere is introducing new actors into the political scene."

Byron York, "KosWorld," *National Review*, April 24, 2006, pp. 40–42. Copyright © 2006 by National Review, Inc., 215 Lexington Avenue, New York, NY 10016. Reproduced by permission.

The Left-Wing Blogosphere Is Divisive

It sounds impressive. And there is no doubt that the bloggers are having an impact. But talks with Democratic strategists and political players suggest it may not be the impact that the bloggers want. At this moment, the left-wing blogosphere is not only the most energetic force inside the Democratic party—it is also the most divisive. The question now is whether it will contribute to Democratic victories in midterm elections this November [2006] or instead end up being the Republicans' not-so-secret weapon as they fight off their own problems and try to keep control of Congress. . . .

At the Daily Kos, anger can go in all directions. And lately a good bit of it has been hitting Democrats. Not long ago, for example, a mainstream Democratic strategist named Steve Elmendorf—he worked extensively with former House minority leader Richard Gephardt—was quoted in the *Washington Post* [as] saying of the liberal blogosphere, "The trick will be to harness their energy and their money without looking like you are a captive of the activist Left." That might not seem a terribly controversial statement, but upon reading it, the activist Left became very, very angry. Calling Elmendorf a "sleazebag amoral lobbyist," Moulitsas threatened to put him out of business. "Here's notice, any Democrat associated with Elmendorf will be outed," Moulitsas wrote. "The netroots can then decide for itself whether it wants to provide some of that energy and money to that candidate."

A threat like that resonates in the Democratic political world, much more so than the anger pointed at Republicans, because Moulitsas and the "netroots" can bring money and buzz to favored candidates—and deny them to non-favored candidates. "The online community collectively can generate $100,000 for a candidate, which is not insignificant," says one Democratic strategist (not Steve Elmendorf) who asked to remain anonymous. "But the paradox is, in order for the community to take sufficient interest in the candidate, the candidate has to do or say something that would make it impossible to win in the district."

The strategist points to the experience of Democrat Paul Hackett in his run for Congress from Ohio's 2nd District. Hackett, a veteran of the Iraq War, loudly called President Bush a "chickenhawk" and, echoing Moulitsas, said "the Republican party has been hijacked by the religious fanatics that, in my opinion, aren't a whole lot different than Osama bin Laden." The left-wing blogosphere cheered wildly and raised thousands of dollars for him. But in the end, Hackett narrowly lost to Republican representative Jean Schmidt, who was widely regarded as a very weak candidate. He later launched an abortive attempt to run for the Senate, but fell victim to his own inexperience and tendency to make extreme statements—the very things the bloggers loved him for. . . .

Democratic politicians fear having the bloggers as enemies; with their energy and their megaphone, they can be the source of endless aggravation.

The left-wing blogosphere's record in picking winners is, in a word, dismal. In the last couple of years, Moulitsas has decided to give special support to a total of 13 Democratic congressional candidates. All of them lost. And that, of course, doesn't count John Kerry in 2004.

Reaching Out to the Blogs

Despite all their defeats, Moulitsas and his allies in the liberal blogosphere are increasingly seen as a force to be reckoned with. Why?

Certainly politicians want the money they can raise. And officeholders aren't in the business of turning down support. But it may be that, more than anything, Democratic politicians fear having the bloggers as enemies; with their energy and their megaphone, they can be the source of endless aggravation.

So increasingly Democratic officeholders and candidates are trying to bring the bloggers inside, to make them feel included—and to blunt their criticisms. For example, in recent months the blogs have been quite angry at House Democratic leader Nancy Pelosi, feeling that she has been ineffective at fighting back against Republicans and fearful that she will support the regulation of political speech on the Internet. In March, the Daily Kos held a poll of its readers asking whether they approved of the job that Pelosi, Senate Democratic leader Harry Reid, and Democratic National Committee chairman Howard Dean were doing. The readers loved Dean; 84 percent approved of his performance. They were so-so on Reid, who scored a 50 percent approval rate. But they couldn't stand Pelosi—just 19 percent approved of her performance.

So now Pelosi has begun to "reach out" to the blogs. "We are talking to them more, we are doing conference calls with them," says a source close to Pelosi who asked not to be named. Pelosi learned that the bloggers were not just angry over Internet regulation; they also felt she should have been more supportive of the anti-war statements of Democratic representative John Murtha, and they wanted her to take a leading role in an ethics crusade against Rep. Bob Ney and other Republicans. Pelosi is as partisan as they come, but that wasn't her way of doing things. "I think there was a real misunderstanding of what we do in the House," the source says. The source also notes that Pelosi is personally not terribly Web-savvy; she doesn't surf the blogs herself and relies on staff to tell her what is in them. She wasn't really aware of how much the netroots types resented her. . . .

The problem with the left-wing blogosphere's approach to politics might not be that they are too far to the left, or too angry, or too eager to be heard. It might be that the combination of all those things makes them self-isolating. Read the Daily Kos and MyDD, as well as other top sites like Atrios, AMERICAblog, Crooks and Liars, Democratic Underground, and FireDogLake, and you'll find a lot of angry statements that can be reduced to this: George W. Bush is a warmonger, or a chickenhawk, or a moron, and Democrats are wimps and weasels for not standing up to him. The first point obviously turns off all Republicans, and the second turns off many Democrats. In the end, the bloggers are left mostly with themselves.

Widely Read Blogs Reach Only a Fraction of the Voters

And that, in political terms, is a pretty small group. Even if the Daily Kos reaches as many people as Moulitsas claims, it's not a huge number when one considers that John Kerry received 60 million votes in 2004 and lost. What the netroots enthusiasts overlook is that the country is so large that its political fringes are big, too—one might create an organization that attracts a million people, or 2 million, and not reach beyond the most intense fraction of the Democratic base.

"You can build your own community on the Net," says Joe Trippi, the former Dean campaign manager who has worked closely with Moulitsas and netroots activists, but it won't necessarily bring you victory. "The Dean campaign was 650,000 people," Trippi says. "You have to have 60 million to be president."

Even if 1 million people read the Daily Kos each week, they're probably the same 1 million who respond to ads from MoveOn.org and listen to Air America radio.

Trippi is a booster of the political uses of the Internet, and he believes it will grow enormously in the future, but he recites an example that illustrates the hazards of such an approach. "If you try to start a rock gardeners' community on-line, I guarantee you, if you become the biggest authority on rock gardens on the Net, then 100,000 or 200,000 people would sign up. If you are passionate about rock gardening, you can build a rock-gardening community."

That is undoubtedly true, but it simply shows that in a country the size of the United States, you can attract a lot of people to even the most esoteric of ideas. And if you attract 200,000 members of the rock-gardening community, what have you got? A significant slice of the American population? Or a bunch of rock-gardening enthusiasts? By the same light, even if 1 million people read the Daily Kos each week, they're probably the same 1 million who respond to ads from Move On.org and listen to Air America radio. That explains a lot about how the Daily Kos can seem so successful and at the same time be so limited.

Not long ago, a political scientist referred to Moulitsas as a "kingmaker." To which another blogger, Mickey Kaus, replied, "Oh yeah? Name the king." The fact is, there is no such king—nor even a member of Congress. Now, surely that will change. Surely in the future at least one Moulitsas-supported candidate will win a campaign. But it will take much more than one victory to make not just Moulitsas, but the entire left-wing blogosphere, into kingmakers. There might not be enough rock gardeners out there to make it happen.

CHAPTER 3

How Are Blogs Affecting American Culture?

Overview: The Impact of Blogging

Robbie Allen

Robbie Allen is a distinguished IT engineer at Cisco Systems. He is the author or coauthor of many books.

In a short span of five years [2001–2005], blogs have invaded our culture and left an indelible mark on society. From politics to journalism, blogs are reshaping our notion of how content is created and information is disseminated.

In 2002, I created a personal website to host supplemental information for books I was writing for O'Reilly Media. My site's front page was just a list of short status updates I'd make from time to time about whatever I was working on. A year after I started the site, some colleagues began referring to it as my "blog". To me, it was just a website I updated periodically.

This raises an interesting question about what constitutes a blog. In simple terms, a blog is just an online journal of sorts. Some are broadly focused and act as an online version of a diary covering all aspects of a person's daily life, while others are narrower and focus on a specific topic area. Blogs began proliferating in the early 2000s due to the advent of blogging software such as Blogger, Wordpress, and Moveable Type. Instead of editing HTML directly as I did with my site, you can use these tools to easily create blog entries via the Web, your mobile phone, and even email.

The term "blog" was coined in 1998 as a derivation of "weblog", but online journals have been around since the early days of the Web. In fact, blogging isn't as much of a technological innovation as it is a social phenomenon. The internet created a platform to enable free flowing communication and information exchange, but it wasn't until blogging hit the mainstream that the web became a medium to capture society's stream of consciousness. People of all backgrounds, interests, and biases now contribute to the global discourse on human affairs.

Blogs have been growing at an incredible rate. Technorati, a leading blog search engine, has been keeping track of the growth in the blogosphere (the collection of blogs) since 2003. According to their stats, the number of blogs has doubled every five months for three straight years. Now [in December 2005] they are tracking over 22 million blogs with 70,000 new blogs being added every day! While only a small percentage of blogs are regularly updated, this explosion in growth has had an interesting impact on a variety of facets of daily life.

Politics

Political blogs are some of the most common blogs in the blogosphere. During the 2004 presidential campaign, Howard Dean became the first presidential candidate to use blogging as a way to reach out to his supporters. Through blogging he was able to establish a loyal following before the traditional media outlets took him seriously. Now, it is common practice for political candidates of all levels to use blogs as a campaign tool.

Corporate America

Just as with politics, it is becoming increasingly common for corporate executives to create blogs in an effort to reach out to customers. In the post-Enron [a major corporation that filed bankruptcy in 2001 and was found to be guilty of fraud] era, blogs help executives appear more approachable and transparent. Especially in high tech companies, it is not uncommon for many executives including CEOs and VPs to have blogs. It isn't clear yet if this is just a fad among executives to demonstrate their technical relevance or if it will continue long-term as a true mechanism for executives and customers to interact.

Blogging as a Business

Blogs have become a big business with a couple of recent blog networks being acquired by large companies. America Online purchased Weblogs, Inc. in October 2005 for an estimated $25 million. Weblogs, Inc. is a network of over 85 blogs covering a variety of topic areas. Now, new blog networks are popping up and it will be interesting to see if the traditional media outlets acquire the popular blog networks much as they did popular content sites in the late 1990s.

For individual blogs, it is a common practice to use Google Adsense as a means to earn money through advertising. While most blogs earn in the tens of dollars per month range, some of the most popular blogs reportedly earn thousands of dollars per month. For my blogs, the advertising revenue I collect covers the expenses of hosting my site with a little left over.

Journalism

In some cases, nationwide news stories have been sparked by bloggers. The recent Sony DRM [digital rights management] fiasco started when security researcher Mark Russinovich posted a blog entry about a malicious rootkit he found on his computer. Bloggers played a key role in outing [news anchor] Dan Rather during Memogate [a scandal involving memos shown on CBS News that proved to be forged]. During Hurricane Katrina, one of the most detailed and widely read survival stories came from a blogger that worked at an internet service provider in New Orleans.

Bloggers outnumber journalists by a large number and are not constrained by deadlines, editors, or fact-checking. As more stories are scooped by bloggers and as more topics are covered than traditional media outlets can get to, the line between journalism and blogging begins to blur. Yahoo! made headlines of their own recently by including blog entries as part of their news portal. This has become the source of intense debate with some arguing that blogging is a form of journalism (i.e., citizen journalism) and others in fierce opposition. Whether blogging fits your definition of journalism, if you respect a blog's author and find the content informative, there is no reason it shouldn't be available right next to traditional news sources in your news portal of choice. Just as with journalism, a blog is only as good as its source (or sources).

Fad or Future?

While blogging has certain fad-like qualities because it is new and cool, I believe we've only seen the beginning. People have been writing their thoughts on the Web for over 10 years, but in the last 5 years blogging has helped legitimize the practice. Is the blogosphere perfect? Definitely not. While it is a great environment to read other people's ideas, those ideas may not always be fact-based, insightful, or politically/culturally correct. However, blogging does provide anyone with access to the web a way to write about anything they want and potentially reach a global audience. This has not been possible in the past and we've only begun to see the consequences. At a minimum, blogging is making our society more transparent and causing an acceleration in the flattening of the world [globalization—the leveling of economic opportunity between nations]. The only real question is when are *you* going to start a blog?

Blogging Significantly Influences Mainstream Journalism

Rebecca MacKinnon

Rebecca MacKinnon is a research fellow at Harvard Law School's Berkman Center for Internet and Society. She is a former CNN Beijing bureau chief and is cofounder of GlobalVoicesOnline, a global citizens' media community.

"Blogging, Journalism, and Credibility: Battleground and Common Ground," a conference held in late January [2005] at Harvard, featured a group of fifty journalists, bloggers, news executives, media scholars and librarians trying to make sense of the new media environment. The relationship between bloggers and journalists was a particular focus. Since the conference, the resignation of CNN's Eason Jordan [who was widely criticized by bloggers for publicly accusing the U.S. military of deliberately targeting journalists for assassination] and the Jeff Gannon [a White House reporter whose journalistic credentials have been questioned] White House scandal have only underscored the power of weblogs as a new form of citizens' media. We are entering an era in which professionals have lost their monopoly over information—not just the reporting of it, but also the framing of what's important for the public to know. Have blogs chipped away at the credibility of mainstream media? How have they influenced the way news is being reported? Is credibility a zero-sum game—in which credibility gained by blogs is lost by mainstream media and vice versa? Conference participants put their minds to these questions, among many others. We've excerpted and abridged some of their thoughts below.

Jay Rosen's Thoughts

So bloggers vs. journalists is over. It doesn't mean that they're not going to fight anymore or that we won't have arguments, or that it's all peace and love or anything like that. In fact, the tension between the two will go on. It's necessary and it's inevitable. But we shouldn't see these two camps as adversaries or enemies or opposites, because if we simply look at what happened with the tsunami story, and the way that independent citizen journalists were able to contribute to that, it's obvious that blogs have some role in journalism. We just have to figure out what that is.

First of all, there has been and there is a power shift going on: from the producers of media to the people formerly known as the audience. That's what I like to call them, because they're not really an audience anymore. And terms like "audience" and "consumer" and "viewer" and "reader"—which have become threaded into journalism—aren't really that accurate for the people on the other end of the process. So there has been a power shift from producers to users, mostly because of the Internet.

> [Professional journalists] have to get used to bloggers and others with an independent voice talking about them, fact-checking them, overlooking them.

Secondly, this has led to a loss of sovereignty in the press. What I mean by that is simply a loss of exclusive control. Areas that once were under the domain of the journalist are now not exclusively under the domain of the journalist. You are not the boss anymore. What you say is not the law.

The third key idea is that because of this power shift, because of the loss of sovereignty, a lot of pressure is being put on mainstream journalism's key Ideas—the ideas and principles that make it what it is. There's pressure on those things, and they haven't been subject to critical examination for a long time. And that is one of the contexts in which blogging has erupted.

Objectivity as an ethical touchstone, as one of my sources said, is faltering in mainstream journalism. It doesn't provide the kind of guidance and direction that it once did. And this is part of the intellectual crisis. Problems of finding a believable voice keep growing in mainstream journalism, and this is related to the shift in power.

Blogging is very well adapted to the world that I describe. It is well adapted to a world where the shift in power is taking place, to a world where there are many centers of sovereignty. Blogging is well adapted to two-way dialogue as opposed to one-to-many dialogue, which is also part of the media shift that we are living through. And of course blogging is not only well adapted but organic to the web and is itself one of the artifacts of the Internet.

So that's why these two things are butted up against each other. As Rebecca Blood, a student of the weblog form, puts it, "Blogging and journalism exist in a shared media space." One of the reasons blogging vs. journalism is over is that nobody is leading that space. So you can just forget it. We have to get used to existing in the same media space—by which we mean bloggers and journalists are there competing for the same scarce resource of attention, addressing the same important issues and able to reach users.

The press is separating from this other big institution called the media and is moving about in social space, so that a lot of the press today is not based anymore in the media—especially the commercial media. Increasingly, because of the Internet, because of blogging, some of the press is actually shifting into public hands. So whereas the press and the media once overlapped almost completely, now the press has shifted.

The nonprofit world owns a piece of it, activists and people involved in politics own a piece of it and the public owns a piece of it.

One of the biggest challenges for professional journalists today is that they have to live in a shared media space. They have to get used to bloggers and others with an independent voice talking about them, fact-checking them, overlooking them—and they no longer have exclusive title to the press. They have to share the press with the public. Rearranging the ideas of journalism to account for that kind of a world is a big challenge. It's very difficult because the ideas that gave birth to professional journalism, the way we teach it and understand it, were in fact an artifact of a one-to-many world. They were built for the media platform that is slowly disintegrating. They are the products of an era of professionalism in American life and modern life that is also slowly passing.

Bloggers are developing the platform that journalists will one day occupy, and that is the reason why people in the mainstream press should pay attention to them.

Journalists have been slow to understand why they owe a debt to bloggers. They owe a debt because the people who are developing the web as a medium for journalism are bloggers and people like them. Those who are discovering its potential—who are developing the tools and the protocols, who are pushing forward the ideas and the practices of web journalism—are not for the most part professional journalists. They are independent authors and bloggers and writers on the web.

So if we look, for example, at what Dave Winer once called "the art of linking." the people who are experts at linking are bloggers. If we look at tapping distributed knowledge around the web, the people who know how to do that are bloggers. If we look at news as conversation, which is such an important metaphor today, the people putting that into practice are bloggers. Bloggers are developing this platform that journalists will one day occupy, and that is the reason why people in the mainstream press should pay attention to them.

Dave Winer's Thoughts

I think I can speak for most, if not all, of the bloggers in the room when I say that we have never woken up thinking about how we can get rid of professional journalists. If anything, we have worked hard to bring them in.

If you want to understand the blogger mentality, think of us as evangelists. We're zealots. We want to bring you in. We want you to use our tools. We want you to learn what we have learned and then make the world a better place. We are the idealists. We are into, you know, truth and justice and so forth. We have a passion for news, and maybe that can act as a reminder to the professionals that somewhere deep inside of your core is that same passion. That's the thing that unites us. That's the bond that we share.

Rather than looking at it as an adversarial relationship, let's look at the ways we can help each other, because God knows we have much bigger problems to solve. Look really, really seriously at how you can adopt practices of blogging in what you do. For example, providing full transcripts of every interview that you do would be something that a lot of your readers would appreciate.

Ed Cone's Thoughts

I am a professional journalist, and I didn't understand blogging until I got a weblog. I thought I understood it. I profiled Dave Winer for *Wired*, and I thought, "Oh, this is neat. I get it." Until I got a weblog and started blogging, I didn't really understand what it meant to do it. So the first thing I would say to journalists who are curious about this is, "You might want to get a weblog. And you can do it anonymously."

Let me report just a little bit about some common ground that has begun to emerge in my hometown. The sort of "aha" moment came about five months ago when [John Robinson,] the editor-in-chief of a substantial regional daily, started his own weblog. What they are doing—and what we, the people of Greensboro, are doing on our own and in parallel and with them—is developing a new kind of media culture. There's a lot of common ground.

If you go to EdCone.com you will see a post this morning about two articles about last night's county commissioner meeting in Gilford County, North Carolina. The newspaper covered the meeting, and they covered it the way they cover meetings. They covered it well, but they focused on a particular issue of interest to the newspaper, which is economic development.

I am a writer and a reporter, and I feel tremendously empowered as a professional by [blogging].

Another guy, a blogger, covered it too, and he focused on other issues. The paper has space constraints. They have to cover a limited amount of what happened at that meeting. Now the reporter Matt Williams can go to his own *News & Record* weblog, link to Sam Heed's coverage and say, "By the way, let me comment on what I couldn't get in the paper. I don't even have to start from scratch and rewrite it. I can just point you to Sam and then take off from there."

And at the same time, we have independent bloggers who want nothing to do with the *News & Record*, and they have created what I call an online alternative media of their own; they're congregating at aggregator sites like greensboro101.com. They are having blog meet-ups. They see themselves as competitors, correctors, potential contributors.

We do not claim to have figured out what is going on any better than anybody else. A lot of folks who are blogging down there are very interested in pushing this forward and working together and working separately, but there is this tendency to say, "Well, you haven't done it yet, so it's a failure. Nobody's making money, so it's a failure."

And I'll go back to what I said originally. I am a writer and a reporter, and I feel tremendously empowered as a professional by this tool.

Blogging Has Replaced the Common Culture with Subcultures

Terry Teachout

Terry Teachout is Commentary's *regular music critic, the drama critic of the* Wall Street Journal, *and the author of several books.*

As a publishing phenomenon, blogs may strike some observers as reminiscent of a development first observed in the early 60's, when "niche" magazines began to supplant mass-circulation titles like *Life* and the *Saturday Evening Post.* But bloggers are not simply imitating the successful marketing strategies of yesterday's editors. Rather, their work is indicative of a sea change in American culture, one that has been accelerated in recent years by the web-based information technologies and "new media" that are now an integral part of the lives of most middle-class Americans.

Goodbye, Common Culture

The simplest description of this change is also the starkest one: the common culture of widely shared values and knowledge that once helped to unite Americans of all creeds, colors, and classes no longer exists. In its place, we now have a "balkanized" group of subcultures whose members pursue their separate, unshared interests in an unprecedented variety of ways.

The idea of a common American culture is so central to the American idea itself that it was long taken for granted. Just as young people pledged allegiance to the American flag in school each day, so they studied the same historical events, read many of the same books, heard the same popular songs on radio, and watched the same movies and TV programs. No one, whether in or out of school, seriously attempted to deny that our country's cultural heritage was that of the Judeo-Christian West, and more specifically of what Winston Churchill called "the English-speaking peoples." Though immigrants from other regions were (mostly) welcomed to our shores, it was assumed that their children, at least, would learn English and adopt Western ways, and so become full-fledged Americans.

At the same time, Western culture remained open to non-Western influence, and America in particular became known for its tendency to absorb immigrant folkways, incorporating them into the common culture and in the process giving them a distinctively American slant. This is the true, now-forgotten meaning of the melting-pot metaphor coined by the playwright Israel Zangwill in 1908: America not only changed its newest citizens, but was changed by them in return. . . .

Warnings that this vision might be under assault from within were first voiced in the 1970's by neo-conservatives (and certain like-minded liberals), who saw a threat to the common culture in the teachings of a new generation of left-wing intellectuals, most of them academics, who were opposed to the traditional understanding of America as a melting pot of ethnic identity. Not until the 80's, however, did their activities come to be more widely seen as a major problem in the making. . . .

As late as 1995, I was complaining in print of the "slowness with which conservative intellectuals have come to grips with the fact that there is a Kulturkampf afoot, and that it is the defining political reality of the post-Soviet era." Calling for a "responsible consensus position on culture," I went on to say: "What is missing from the present-day American political scene is a Ronald Reagan of culture: a 'great communicator' who can dramatize the perils of balkanization, present an affirmative vision of America's common culture, and thereby lead the way back from the brink."

Like a baseball game called on account of rain, America's culture war was called on account of obsolescence.

Earlier [in 2005], I was bemused to find my words reprinted on The American Scene (www.theamericanscene.com), a blog written by a group of young conservatives. At first I was unable to recall the occasion on which I had written them, and even after remembering, I found it all but impossible to think myself back into the mind-set that had produced so apocalyptic a formulation. Not only had no one remotely resembling a "Ronald Reagan of culture" come along in the ensuing decade, but the very idea of a "responsible consensus position on culture" now sounded alien to me.

To be sure, I had not changed my mind about the significance of Western culture, or the dangers of the radical relativism preached by the academics of the 80's. But something else had happened in the meantime: like a baseball game called on account of rain, America's culture war was called on account of obsolescence.

"We do not nowadays refute our predecessors, we pleasantly bid them goodbye," George Santayana wrote in *Character and Opinion in the United States*. In such manner did Americans, contrary to all expectation, bid goodbye to the common culture that had once united them. Indeed, they seemed almost indifferent to—or unaware of—its collapse. . . .

Decline of Mainstream Media

Until very recently, the mainstream media [MSM] had a monopoly on the dissemination of information to large numbers of Americans. News was what the MSM said it was, and nothing more. This began to change in the late 90's, when the earliest blogs appeared on the web. It was natural that conservatives, alienated as they were from the MSM, should have embraced blogging so promptly and enthusiastically. Especially in the wake of 9/11, when a host of amateur political commentators took to the Web to write in support of the war on terror, the readership of such right-of-center "warblogs" as andrewsullivan.com and Little Green Footballs (www.littlegreenfootballs.com) grew dramatically. Left-of-center blogs were slower to catch on, but they are now as popular, if not as numerous as their conservative and libertarian counterparts.

By 2003, the year I started [my arts blog] About Last Night, the mainstream media were finally taking reluctant note of political blogs, and 2004 saw a spectacular demonstration of their coming-of-age. Dan Rather, anchorman of the *CBS Evening News* since 1981, was forced into retirement when right-wing bloggers, none of them a journalist in the traditional sense of the word, discovered that a potentially damaging report about President [George W.] Bush's National Guard service, for which Rather was in part responsible, had apparently been based on forged documents. The MSM initially chose not to cover this story, but the blogosphere decided that it was news—and thereby made it news.

Rather's demise was one sign of the breakup of the big-media information monopoly. Another can be seen in the fast-declining circulation of American newspapers—down 13 percent since the peak year of 1984—and the shrunken ratings of nightly network TV newscasts, which are now viewed by 28.8 million people, down from 52.1 million a quarter-century ago. At the same time, more and more Americans, especially those in their thirties and younger, are turning away from the MSM—only 23 percent between the ages of eighteen and twenty-nine read newspapers—to embrace the new Web-based media, which offer a proliferating variety of points of view and styles of communication.

Even when they read print-media stories, moreover, Web-oriented Americans tend to find them by going to blogs and other websites whose proprietors pick and choose at will from the MSM's offerings, linking to some stories and ignoring others according to their political inclinations. To "get the news" through the prism of a left-wing blog like Daily Kos or right-wing websites like Lucianne.com (www.lucianne.com) or RealClear Politics (www.realclearpolitics.com), all of which offer links to stories originally posted on the sites of such liberal newspapers as the *New York Times* and the *Washington Post*, is a very different experience from reading those newspapers themselves.

> *What began as the ultimate outsider activity . . . is turning into the same insider's game played by the old establishment media the bloggerati love to critique.*

Rupert Murdoch, the founder and chairman of News Corporation, recently summed up the implications of these developments in a speech to the American Society of Newspaper Editors:

What is happening right before us is, in short, a revolution in the way young people are accessing news. They don't want to rely on the morning paper for their up-to-date information. They don't want to rely on a godlike figure from above to tell them what's important. And to carry the religion analogy a bit further, they certainly don't want news presented as gospel.

Instead, they want their news on demand, when it works for them. They want control over their media, instead of being controlled by it. They want to question, to probe, to offer a different angle.

What Murdoch did not say, but could have said, is that a country whose citizens live in culturally separate geographic enclaves, send their children to culturally separate schools, and get their news from culturally separate media is a country without a common culture. That is why the American Kulturkampf petered out some time around the turn of the 21st century. Instead of staying to fight, Americans withdrew from the battleground, went home to cultivate their own cultural gardens—and started blogging. . . .

How the Blogsphere Differs from the Culture of the Past

As has often been remarked, blogging is an amateur culture in the exact sense of the word. Even those bloggers who are artistic or intellectual professionals of one kind or another are motivated chiefly by love of the things they write about. And whereas journalism in America has come to be regarded as a "profession" open only to trained, credentialed specialists, life in the blogosphere more closely resembles the European notion of journalism as a skill that can be practiced by anyone who knows how to write and has something to say. . . .

When newspapers do become obsolete . . . it will be because their functions have been taken over by a variety of Web-based media that can do them better.

What began as the ultimate outsider activity—a way to break the newspaper and TV stranglehold on the gathering and dissemination of information—is turning into the same insider's game played by the old establishment media the bloggerati love to critique. The more blogs you read and the more often you read them, the more obvious it is: they've fallen in love with themselves, each other, and the beauty of what they're creating. The cult of media celebrity hasn't been broken by the Internet's democratic tendencies; it's just found new enabling technology. . . .

How *else* does the culture archipelago differ from the city-based cultural enclaves of the past? Above all, it is decentralized to the point of atomization. Its "citizens" rarely meet face to face, nor do they flock to performing-arts centers at appointed hours or read mass-circulation newspapers and middlebrow magazines. Instead, they pursue their own specialized interests, intensely but also narrowly, making use of web-based electronic media that are available, as the saying goes, "24/7." If they cannot get what they want when they want it, they need only change the channel.

This sped-up cycle of cultural supply and demand was pungently characterized by Richard Brookhiser in a column occasioned by Rupert Murdoch's recent speech: "Murdoch was being polite. What he was telling his colleagues was: newspapers are dead.". . .

For all the contempt in which they affect to hold the mainstream media, too many bloggers remain in their thrall, complaining about what the media do wrong instead of figuring out how to do other things right.

When newspapers do become obsolete—which will happen sooner rather than later—it will be because their functions have been taken over by a variety of Web-based media that can do them better. (Blogs, for example, are already superseding op-ed pages.) A few existing papers will rise to the challenge and transform themselves into online publications, reconceived in such a way as to take advantage of the unique properties of the Web. Most, however, will not, since established institutions rarely if ever transform themselves, least of all in response to external threats to their survival. Instead, they are replaced by new institutions that spring up in response to those same threats, seeing them as opportunities for long-overdue change.

But as Brookhiser's description also implies, the culture archipelago is no utopia, any more than was America in the fast-receding days of the common culture. Nor are blogs alone capable of replacing newspapers, or even magazines, notwithstanding the triumphalist fantasies of certain bloggers with overactive imaginations.

Blogs Have Limitations

Blogs, after all, have their own built-in limitations. Chief among these is a tendency toward superficiality. While a blogger can write at any length, few seem inclined to post the kind of full-length essay that is the stock in trade of an intellectual magazine like *Commentary*. Most favor brief, suggestive postings that imply more than they state, and they no less typically prefer hit-and-run assertion to detailed argument, verbal slugfests to coolly reasoned refutations. Moreover, for all the contempt in which they affect to hold the mainstream media, too many bloggers remain in their thrall, complaining about what the media do wrong instead of figuring out how to do other things right.

These limitations, however, matter only to those who see the blog as a substitute for an existing medium, rather than as a new medium that does new things in new ways. I do not look to About Last Night as an outlet for my extended essays. Those I continue to publish in *Commentary* and other print magazines while also linking to them on my blog, which I use as a "portal" through which interested people can find out about the full range of my work as a writer and commentator. Such "portals," made possible by the fact that most newspapers and magazines (*Commentary* among them) now also publish their content on linkable websites, are a good example of something blogs do that could not have been done, or even imagined, prior to their invention.

Similarly, About Last Night allows me to post spontaneously and immediately in response to newsworthy events: the death of an artist, the announcement of a major literary award, a performance from which I have just returned. Just as important, it allows me to decide which of these events are newsworthy, rather than having to talk an editor into letting me write about them, or being talked by an editor into writing about them, often days or weeks after the fact.

No less unique to blogging is its potential for interactivity. . . .

Bloggers converse not only with their readers but with one another, remarking on postings that interest them. A posting that draws the attention of other bloggers, whether favorable or otherwise, can circulate throughout the blogosphere in a matter of hours.

This interactivity appears at first glance to contradict the atomizing tendencies of blogging. In fact, both things are intrinsic to the nature of the culture archipelago, and of the news media in general. Because they are so radically decentralized, blogs inevitably tend to pull us apart—yet they also facilitate the formation of personal associations that need not be limited by considerations of geography. . . .

A New Kind of Common Culture?

Artblogs are barely more than three years old. It is far too soon to say which of their opposing tendencies, the atomizing or the embracing, will have a more profound effect on the wider culture they have already started to shape. It may be that blogging will encourage the creation of a new kind of common culture, exerting something of the same unifying force as did the old middlebrow media (and as About Last Night seeks to do). Or not: if the experience of political blogs is any indication, blogging may be more likely to foster discrete subcultures of shared interest, larger and more cohesive but nonetheless separate.

The question then becomes whether the memberships of these subcultures will overlap to any substantial degree. I think they will—that, in fact, they already do. . . .

No doubt there will always be shouting in the blogosphere, but it need not all be past each other.

One thing of which I am sure is that the common culture of my youth is gone for good. It was hollowed out by the rise of ethnic "identity politics," then splintered beyond hope of repair by the emergence of the web-based technologies that so maximized and facilitated cultural choice as to make the broad-based offerings of the old mass media look bland and unchallenging by comparison. For all the nostalgia with which I look back on the days of the Top 40, the Book-of-the-Month Club, and The Ed Sullivan Show, I prefer to make my own cultural decisions, and I welcome the ease with which the new media permit me to do so.

At the same time, however, I still feel the need for a common space in which Americans can come together to talk about the things that matter to us all. And so my hope is that the blogosphere, for all its fissiparous [divisive] tendencies, will evolve over time into just such a space. No doubt there will always be shouting in the blogosphere, but it need not all be past each other. When the history of blogging is written a half-century from now, its chroniclers may yet record that the highest achievement of the Internet, a seemingly impersonal piece of postmodern technology, turned out to be its unprecedented ability to bring creatures of flesh and blood closer together.

Blogs Provide Responses to Community Issues

Craig Colgan

Craig Colgan is a Washington, D.C., writer and contributor to the Washington Post *and* National Journal. *He is also the former associate editor of* American School Board Journal, *where the following viewpoint first appeared. His Web site is www.craigcolgan.com.*

Florida's Pinellas County Schools endured a brutal 2004–05 school year. Two students died—one in October and the other in February—after they were struck by vehicles moments after stepping off school buses.

In March, police were called to a Pinellas school, where they handcuffed an unruly 5-year-old student as a teacher videotaped the entire episode. The *St. Petersburg Times* acquired the tape and placed it on its website for all to see. Soon national news media were running the story and the tape.

And other issues simmered as well, including a continuing controversy over desegregation and the district's student assignment plan.

The community's response to all of the above struck more than one note, and the volume at times was high. But amid the emotion could be found plenty of perceptive insight and clear-eyed suggestions.

How do we know about the community's response? We can read an important slice of it on a website called The Classroom. Written by Clayton Wilcox, the district's superintendent, The Classroom is a blog—a fast-create, fast-reply site that, in times of high emotion, can quickly become a must-read for parents, politicians, and community leaders.

Located at www.sptimes.com/classroom, the blog—or "weblog," to use the quickly fading original term—is posted on the *Times* website. Judging by the passionate, often detailed reader comments, it's a hit.

The key question is whether schools want to speak to constituents, or speak with them using this technology.

In one posting, Wilcox asked the community to react to the handcuffing incident and to the video. More than 400 comments were posted within 24 hours, says Kevin McGeever, city editor of sptimes.com. McGeever removed a few comments that were profane or otherwise coarse, and wrote an item on the blog two days later explaining the deletions. His posting inspired an additional 830 comments within a week.

Wilcox's post beginning that sequence seems innocent enough, but given that he is superintendent of a 114,000-student school district, it also could be called fearless. "Please know that the police were there at the request of school staff," the superintendent wrote. "It is not our position or my intention to judge their actions. . . . I simply am asking you for your reactions to the video and for your suggestions as to how we can deal with future incidents like this one."

What's revolutionary about this tool is that it puts give-and-take into Web publishing.

The word "we" captures much of the power of a tool that finally makes the Internet truly accessible. "It has been very powerful," says Wilcox of his new blog. "And it's cool."

Blogging—a Short History

This is a story of potential—not of how K–12 administrators and school board members are flocking to blogging. They aren't. School leaders tend not to be "early adopters" of new technology.

"With the incredible time pressures that face upper-level managers in education, it's not always possible for them to take the time to stay abreast of these kinds of developments and see their potential," says Kim Cavanaugh, technology administrator for the Palm Beach County, Fla., school district, who regularly explores Web design issues on his own blog at www.brainfrieze.net.

Today, almost anyone with rudimentary computer skills can establish a surprisingly sophisticated space on the Web within minutes.

And when an important goal of the technology in question is to pave the way for education leaders to easily reach out to their schools, constituents, and communities, another barrier often becomes evident.

"The key question is whether schools want to speak to constituents, or speak with them using this technology," says Will Richardson, a self-described "blogvangelist" who maintains weblogg-ed.com, a site dedicated to discussions about the use of Web-related technologies in K–12 education.

One strength of blogs "is the ability to carry on asynchronous conversations," says Richardson, who is supervisor of instructional technology and communications at Hunterdon Central Regional High School in Flemington, N.J. Richardson believes that "mostly good" can result from these discussion forums but recognizes that the concept "scares a lot of superintendents and administrators."

"I'm amazed people don't get it," Jeff Weiner, senior vice president of Yahoo!, told *Business Week* in a May [2005] cover story on blogs. "Never in the history of market research has there been a tool like this."

What's revolutionary about this tool is that it puts give-and-take into Web publishing. Before blogging, the Web was pretty much a one-way street. Some distant, technologically advanced entity would create Web content, and the rest of us would wander from site to site viewing it. We might buy a book at Amazon.com or vote in an online poll, but mostly we consumed content others produced. We did not create it or benefit directly from the Web's ability to share it quickly.

Blogs have broken that chain. Today, almost anyone with rudimentary computer skills can establish a surprisingly sophisticated space on the Web within minutes. The one-way highway is now two way.

"Weblogs enable the 'read-write Web' to happen," says Thor Prichard, president and CEO of blog developer Clarity Innovations, using the technical term that describes this evolution.

And what a change it has been, in a relatively short period of time. The Pew Internet & American Life Project recently reported that 7 percent of the 120 million adult Internet users in the United States have created blogs. In 2004 alone, blog readership jumped 58 percent.

Teens Leading the Way

Gaining widespread attention in today's mainstream news media are blogs written largely by people who analyze and sometimes break news. Businesses now use blogs to reach out to and cajole their customers, respond immediately to rumors, and build their brands. Almost all major political campaigns have blogs that work to build volunteer and donor lists and spin the news.

A growing number of teachers write in-depth diary blogs about the challenges, rewards, and agonies of their jobs.

But the potential for blogs goes way beyond these few established uses, and teens are leading the charge. Teens—who represent half of all bloggers, according to one study—use blogs to explore hobbies and link to interesting or fun websites. Many are using their own blogs to socialize across the Internet, and more are using them in classrooms, as teachers find new ways to explore the form's potential for learning.

A growing number of teachers write in-depth diary blogs about the challenges, rewards, and agonies of their jobs in personal and powerful fashion, and parent and community groups are catching on as well. One such group, Don't Underestimate Mecklenburg Parents, started its blog (www.dumpcms.com) as it pushed for change on a host of issues in North Carolina's Charlotte-Mecklenburg Schools. Marc Borbely, a former Washington, D.C., teacher, started a blog (www.fixourschools.net) to draw attention to D.C. school buildings that are deteriorating. Borbely's site features photos from outside contributors.

"I happen to think it's a model that should exist in other branches of government too—a public tracking system, where neighbors can document problems and then help each other lobby for change," Borbely says.

With blogs growing in popularity, where does that leave others in the greater K–12 universe, namely superintendents, administrators, principals, and school board members? There may be few bloggers among this group, but those who are involved in this new form of communication say it's a useful, simple, but compelling tool.

I Want to Elevate the Discourse

Florence Johnson, president of the Buffalo, N.Y., school board, maintains a polished blog called A Permanent Revolution. Its mission is spelled out under the name: "Because real educational reform doesn't just happen at weekly school board meetings. We need a continual dialogue to effect dramatic change."

Most of the brief items on the site, found at www.fix education.blogspot.com, are illustrated with color photos and point to online articles and ideas on urban education. Johnson, who calls blogging her "new-found passion," sometimes comments on issues in her district but is careful when she does so. Links alongside her blog point to several Buffalo-based bloggers and advocacy organizations.

"In my travels locally, I noticed that there were pockets of people with really good ideas having these discrete discussions about how to make education better in our city: what other cities were doing, what we were doing wrong and, occasionally what we were doing right," Johnson says. "But the conversation was distributed—it wasn't and still isn't centralized."

Johnson, who was introduced to blogs by her son, loves the freedom they provide. She uses hers to promote important ideas, points of view, and opinions.

"I really want to elevate the local discourse, which is to say I don't deal with tactical issues and concerns. That's my day job," Johnson says with a chuckle. "Many of my colleagues read it regularly. Local education advocates read it. Teachers and administrators read it. And members of the business community read it, which surprised me. It's very encouraging. I think other school board members should try it."

Johnson began her blog just this year [2005]. Only a few education leaders have been at it for any length of time.

One veteran education blogger is Tim Lauer, principal of Lewis Elementary School in Portland, Ore. Lauer, who has worked with blogs at his school for five years, publishes his internal staff bulletin on a password-protected section of the school website, instead of sending it around as an e-mail or on paper. Lewis Elementary's website, www.lewiselementary .org. is arranged like several blogs in one in an organized and cleanly designed format. It sports an events calendar and a weekly public group blog from teachers about their classes' activities.

"The weblog tools give me the opportunity to share content with my community and at the same time keep an archive of that content," Lauer says. "It's just one of many ways that schools can work to be more connected with their communities."

Blogging offers plenty of ways, for example, to republish or "syndicate" content from one blog to another, automatically. "We developed a method for disseminating announcements from a district weblog to each school's internal weblog, all without crowding someone's e-mail inbox or relying on human intervention for it to take place," says Prichard of Clarity Innovations.

While blogs are gaining ground as a communications tool, some predict that administrators and K–12 decision makers will not use them on a widespread basis.

Blogging also offers a channel for more intimate communication. Joyce Hooper, principal at J.H. House Elementary School in Conyers, Ga., started blogging after she was intrigued by a pilot project involving her fifth-grade students. Hooper's blog is written directly to her students, as she discourses on important subjects such as character education.

"Although I greet the students and chat with many of them every morning and wave good-bye every afternoon as they board the buses to go home, I don't feel that I really know how they feel about things or what some of their concerns might be," Hooper says. "Blogging is another avenue of communication with them."

Candor Spurs Discussion

Pinellas County's education blog got its start at the newspaper. Staff members working for the *St. Petersburg Times* website came up with the idea of creating a blog and handing it over to Wilcox, who became superintendent in Pinellas County in November 2004. McGeever, the online city editor who monitors the superintendent's blog, says the staff knew Wilcox was "pretty Web savvy" and that he had the one characteristic that could make the effort a success.

"He is a very candid guy," McGeever says.

Wilcox began in March by posting short, single-paragraph items a couple of times a week, asking for input on important issues. At one point, he even used the blog to break some important news about the district's school choice plans. His host newspaper had to write a story on the topic after Wilcox scooped the newsroom.

"As a newspaper we have hosted two vice presidential debates," McGeever says. "This is analogous to that, an online version of setting up a discussion, bringing the participants together and saying, 'Have at it.' [Wilcox] said he was getting 600 to 700 e-mails a day. With one response on the blog, he can reply to many of those all at once."

Wilcox says he enjoys reading the blog as much as writing it. "It allows me to see trends and opinion waves and sidestep them before I am swallowed up," he says. "People who are offering comments are passionate and caring. I am pleased that people are participating. I wish that more would. It is interesting that some people have even self-appointed themselves moderators of certain strands, but that is the virtual community."

The Pinellas blog is one of several new technologies Wilcox is using to engage the community. Another is the use of handheld devices to provide instant feedback on issues during community forums.

"The blog is just one tool." Wilcox says. "I started it to encourage discussion about improving our schools. We have a lot of work to do to improve education outcomes for kids. And we can't be successful doing that unless we can communicate."

Students and adults have replied to and linked to the blog, as have a number of educators from outside the district and even outside the country. Sometimes Wilcox, instead of posting to the blog's front page, adds his thoughts directly into the comments section of an individual discussion.

One comment from a reader of Wilcox's blog points to the value, the potential, and the difficulty all at once: "Thank you for opening the gate to Oz to parents and the community."

An Unrealized Potential

While blogs are gaining ground as a public engagement tool, some predict that administrators and K–12 decision makers will not use them on a widespread basis. Near the top of their list of reasons is fear of fast feedback.

Parents ultimately are the key to expanding the blog universe into schools.

"Blogs can be places to have honest, open dialogue about issues of the day," says Anne Davis of the Instructional Technology Center at Georgia State University, who trained Hooper and her students on the use of blogs. "Change can come from good discussions, and when the discussion is public you are inviting the input of others. But weblogs are not typical websites most people are used to using. It takes time to see the potential."

Cavanaugh, the technology administrator for the Palm Beach County, Fla., district, says parents ultimately are the key to expanding the blog universe into schools.

"In the end, as much as we tech enthusiasts embrace new technologies, the real pressure for using these tools on the Web will have to come from parents," Cavanaugh says. "Once parents begin to turn up the heat on administrators to provide easier-to-access information, in the same way parents can get so many other types of news and information, then there will be a change."

Blogs Can Impact Grassroots Politics

Lakshmi Chaudhry

Lakshmi Chaudhry has been a reporter and an editor for independent publications for more than six years and is a senior editor at In These Times, *where she covers the intersection of culture and politics.*

"We have no interest in being anti-establishment," says Matt Stoller, a blogger at the popular Web site MyDD.com. "We're going to be the establishment."

That kind of flamboyant confidence has become the hallmark of blog evangelists who believe that blogs promise nothing less than a populist revolution in American politics. In 2006, at least some of that rhetoric is becoming reality. Blogs may not have replaced the Democratic Party establishment, but they are certainly becoming an integral part of it. In the wake of John Kerry's defeat in the 2004 presidential elections, many within the Democratic leadership have embraced blog advocates' plan for political success, which can be summed up in one word: netroots.

This all-encompassing term loosely describes an online grassroots constituency that can be targeted through Internet technologies, including e-mail, message boards, RSS feeds [summaries of frequently updated content from blogs and Web sites] and, of course, blogs, which serve as organizing hubs. In turn, these blogs employ a range of features—discussion boards, Internet donations, live e-chat, social networking tools like MeetUp, online voting—that allow ordinary citizens to participate in politics, be it supporting a candidate or organizing around a policy issue. Compared to traditional media, blogs are faster, cheaper, and most importantly, interactive, enabling a level of voter involvement impossible with television or newspapers.

No wonder, then, that many in Washington are looking to blogs and bloggers to counter the overwhelming financial and ideological muscle of the right—especially in an election year. Just 18 months ago [in 2005] the *New York Times Magazine* ran a cover story depicting progressive bloggers as a band of unkempt outsiders, thumbing their nose at party leadership. But now, it's the party leaders themselves who are blogging. Not only has Senate Minority leader Harry Reid started his own blog—Give 'em Hell Harry—and a media "war room" to "aggressively pioneer Internet outreach," he's also signed up to be the keynote speaker at the annual conference of the top political blog, Daily Kos.

Stoller predicts that as an organizing tool, "blogs are going to play the role that talk radio did in 1994, and that church networks did in 2002."

Blogs ... have the potential to become engines of truly democratic, bottom-up, issue-rich political participation.

An Internet-fueled victory at the polls would certainly be impressive—no candidate backed by the most popular progressive blogs has yet won an election. But electoral success may merely confirm the value of blogs as an effective organizing tool to conduct politics as usual, cementing the influence of a select group of bloggers who will likely be crowned by the media as the new kingmakers. . . .

Can the Netroots Grow the Grassroots?

If television made politics more elitist and less substantive, blogs—and more broadly, netroots tools—have the potential to become engines of truly democratic, bottom-up, issue-rich political participation.

Blogs allow rank-and-file voters to pick the candidate to support in any given electoral race, influence his or her platform, and volunteer their time, money and expertise in more targeted and substantive ways. Democratic candidates in the midterm elections are already busy trying to position themselves as the next Howard Dean [2004 blogger-fave presidential candidate], vying for a digital stamp of approval that will bring with it free publicity, big money and, just maybe, a whole lot of voters.

When Rep. Sherrod Brown (D-Ohio) decided to take on Iraq veteran Paul Hackett in the Democratic primary for the Senate race in Ohio, he moved quickly to neutralize his opponent's advantage as the unquestioned hero of the progressive bloggers. The ace up Brown's sleeve: Jerome Armstrong, founder of the influential MyDD.com and veteran of Howard Dean's online campaign. Brown's next move was a blog entry on The Huffington Post titled, "Why I am a Progressive."

But not everyone is convinced that blogs can be as influential in a midterm election, when there are a large number of electoral contests spread across the country. "Raising money at a nationwide level for a special election is one thing," Pew scholar Michael Cornfield says, "but raising it and developing a core of activists and all the ready-to-respond messages when you have to run hundreds of races simultaneously—which is what will happen in 2006—is another thing." Moreover, the ability of the Internet to erase geographical distances can become a structural weakness in elections where district lines and eligibility are key.

An effective netroots strategy in 2006 will also have to master the shortcomings of Dean's campaign, which stalled mainly because it failed to grow his support base beyond his online constituency—antiwar, white and high-income voters. In contrast, the Bush/Cheney operation used the Internet to coordinate on-the-ground events such as house parties, and rallies involving church congregations.

Cornfield describes the Republican model as, "one person who is online and is plugged into the blogosphere. That person becomes an e-precinct captain, and is responsible for reaching out offline or any means necessary for ten people."

This time around, Armstrong is determined to match the GOP's success. GrowOhio.org, which he describes as "a community blog for Democratic Party activists," will coordinate field operations for not just Brown but all Democratic candidates in each of Ohio's 88 counties. Its primary goal is to reach rural voters in areas where the campaign cannot field organizers on the ground.

"This isn't just about using the net for communications and fundraising, but for field organizing," Armstrong says.

Amateur Detectives Use Blogs to Investigate Crime

Laura Bauer

Laura Bauer is a reporter for the Kansas City Star.

By the time authorities pulled Jodi Sanderholm's car from a lake in south-central Kansas [in January 2007] a swarm of strangers on the Internet had immersed themselves in her story.

They sat at computers across the country and speculated on what happened to the Cowley College student. They played detective, with one Kansan writing from Arkansas City, Kan., about what police were doing and how the town felt. They shared gossip and theories, Internet findings and secondhand news about Sanderholm's disappearance.

"They just pulled the car out on the news," one person wrote around 5 p.m. Tuesday.

As the nation's fascination with crime escalates ... focus blogs often generate more Internet traffic than news stories produce.

"Praying Jodi isn't in the car," wrote another.

They call this cybersleuthing, and some contributors fancy themselves armchair detectives. Whatever the true-crime story of the day, or cold case of the moment, many log on to various sites where accurate information mixes with opinion, some conjecture and half-truths.

As the nation's fascination with crime escalates, and popular nightly television news shows highlight the offense of the day, these focus blogs often generate more Internet traffic than news stories produce. People who feel helpless when a crime occurs can be involved and connected.

Police agencies admit they monitor these blogs, which can muddy the process of determining what's true.

"People feel powerless," said blogger Steve Huff, whose CrimeBlog.US reported Sanderholm's case for several days after her disappearance. "They want to feel like they are doing something about it."

Fact Mixes with Fiction

The bad news is no one filters the information, so fact typically mixes with fiction. Rumors spread easily.

Police agencies admit they monitor these blogs, which can muddy the process of determining what's true.

The good news, though: The blogs do generate information, some of it useful.

"There's this mystique of the detective, the Sherlock Holmes who comes in cold and figures out who done it," said Ken Novak, associate professor of criminal Justice at the University of Missouri–Kansas City. "The reality is that that type of investigation is exceedingly rare. Police rely on information from the public. . . . Gossip and poor information is sometimes better than none."

The Sanderholm case isn't the only breaking news story from the Midwest that consumed bloggers and blog readers [that week].

Immediately after the mainstream media reported [on a] Friday that Ben Ownby had been found in an apartment in Kirkwood, Mo., with Shawn Hornbeck, who was kidnapped in 2002, Huff posted the news on his blog. And the bloggers and contributors went to work, searching sex offender registries across the nation for suspect Michael Devlin's name, gathering various news articles and scouring personal Web pages for new information.

By late Friday afternoon, Huff's blog had linked to the personal web page of a "Shawn Devlin" from Kirkwood, Mo., and a comment written on the ShawnHorbeck.com guestbook in December 2005 by a person of the same name.

"How long are you planning to look for your son?" wrote "Shawn Devlin" on Dec. 1, 2005. Several hours later, the young man posted again, apologizing for what he had written and telling the parents he wanted to write a poem in honor of their son.

On Sunday, Huff informed his readers that the Ownby/Hornbeck story logged more than 100,000 page loads through his site in a 24-hour period, several times the amount of most of his featured stories.

During the investigation of serial killer BTK, Kansas authorities monitored blogs and Web pages to see what information was out there, said Kyle Smith, a spokesman for the Kansas Bureau of Investigation [KBI]. They also watched to see if the killer himself was communicating on the Internet.

People Connect with Crime Stories

Huff, who lives near Atlanta, first posted Sanderholm's story on his CrimeBlog.US two days after she disappeared. From his two years of true-crime blogging, Huff believed the story was one people would connect with.

Sanderholm disappeared Jan. 5 after grabbing lunch at the Subway restaurant in Arkansas City. The freshman, a member of the college's dance team, had been a valedictorian at Arkansas City High School a year before. She was known as a responsible young woman.

"This happened in a place where things don't happen like this," said Huff, who initially got into blogging as a way to tell stories and likes the challenge of getting information others don't have. "On one hand, you have a mystery; on the other, a cautionary tale. I sometimes think people need to be reminded it can happen anywhere."

From 2 to 3 p.m. [the next] Tuesday, more than 1,200 visitors went to Huff's blog. By Wednesday, several other bloggers had linked to his site. More first-time viewers, many from Kansas and some who knew Sanderholm, had logged on.

"I just went by her parents shop," wrote "Kas from Ark City" about 10 a.m. Sunday, two days after Sanderholm disappeared. "The windows are filled with pink posters and printed photos of Jodi. Balloons are tied out front."

These Internet chats can do what other media can't, said Laura James, a lawyer whose blog is Historic True Crime.

"Blogs have the time and space to go into a case in great detail," James said. "And since so many cases now have an Internet component to them . . . it's logical to look to the Web for details about certain news stories."

But people who post on blogs can say whatever they want, Novak said.

Armchair Quarterbacking

Before Sanderholm's body was found and word spread about a possible suspect who had been known to stalk the dance team, those on the blog offered up other possibilities. In another instance, a commenter wrote that investigators had found Sanderholm's clothes, something the media had not yet reported.

"You get speculation, wild theories," said Smith, with the KBI. "Sometimes there are leaks of information you don't want out."

Novak said the blogs also can lead to "armchair quarterbacking" and undeserved criticism toward law enforcement.

"Going through it, it's not that easy," Novak said. "People are probably fast to use 20/20 hindsight, 'You should have known that—it was right there on the blog.'"

Still, Huff said, "bloggers can fill in gaps and at least keep people aware."

Those hungry for information in the Sanderholm case used Huff's blog to keep informed in the hours before her body was found. A relative of the family wrote in to ask people to pray.

Some sent condolences to the family and to each other.

Wrote one contributor:

"Steve I really appriciate (sic) you making a site like this for people to share ideas and vent to one another."

CHAPTER 4

What Ethical and Legal Issues Are Raised by Blogs?

Chapter Preface

For the most part, blogs are used constructively both by their authors and by their readers. However, there is an inherent danger in a medium that permits anyone to say whatever they choose to say, because a few people are likely to abuse the opportunity and thereby spoil it for the majority who want only to express sincere opinions.

Among the issues that have arisen during the rise of blogging is a growing problem with readers—many of them anonymous—who leave inappropriate comments, such as those that harass others, are libelous, or are deliberate falsehoods. This is worse than the annoying childish behavior that has always plagued online forums. Lies can permanently damage innocent people's reputations. Moreover, some bloggers have actually had to quit blogging on account of the harassment and violent threats they have received.

Some people feel that there should be rules to control the posting of abusive comments. Early in 2007 Tim O'Reilly, a well-known publisher and promoter of interactive Web technology, proposed a code of conduct for bloggers that he hoped would ensure online civility. He suggested that bloggers should take responsibility not only for what they write, but for the comments posted in their blogs by others, which would mean posting a warning that objectionable postings will not be tolerated and deleting any that appear. He also suggested that anonymous postings be banned. In addition, he advised ignoring trolls (provocative remarks intended solely to draw an angry response). "As one person advised me long ago when I got in a public tussle with a blog bully," he wrote, "'Never wrestle with a pig. You both get dirty, but the pig likes it.'" Among his other recommendations were that bloggers confront abusers offline when possible, and that they never say anything online that they would not say in person.

O'Reilly called his listing of rules a draft, and he intended that the code be voluntary. Bloggers, he suggested, could post a graphic "badge" on their sites if they adhered to it; those who did not could use a badge that meant "anything goes." It might be thought that most would want to rule out bad conduct, although there would be no way such a code could be enforced, and he did receive a good deal of response from supporters. However, to his surprise, O'Reilly's proposal aroused a storm of protest.

To many bloggers, the issue was one of free speech. Any policy of deleting comments would be censorship, they maintained, and the idea of censorship on the Web was unacceptable. Furthermore, they resented being told by someone else how they should run their blogs. It was pointed out that the people causing the problems would not adhere to the code anyway, while the blameless majority would lose the freedom that is the most prized feature of online interaction.

Together with Jimmy Wales, the creator of the online encyclopedia *Wikipedia*, O'Reilly elaborated on the draft code and suggested making portions of it optional. But they were unable to obtain any consensus. The debate was widely reported by the media for a few weeks before the proposal was quietly dropped. It is unlikely that bloggers will ever agree to a formal system of controlling online behavior. Individually, however, many do take steps to discourage abusiveness, and O'Reilly's idea provoked a good deal of thoughtful discussion about the direction in which online interaction is heading.

Sexual Threats Stifle Some Female Bloggers

Ellen Nakashima

Ellen Nakashima is a staff writer for the Washington Post.

A female freelance writer who blogged about the pornography industry was threatened with rape. A single mother who blogged about "the daily ins and outs of being a mom" was threatened by a cyber-stalker who claimed that she beat her son and that he had her under surveillance. Kathy Sierra, who won a large following by blogging about designing software that makes people happy, became a target of anonymous online attacks that included photos of her with a noose around her neck and a muzzle over her mouth.

As women gain visibility in the blogosphere, they are targets of sexual harassment and threats. Men are harassed too, and lack of civility is an abiding problem on the Web. But women, who make up about half the online community, are singled out in more starkly sexually threatening terms—a trend that was first evident in chat rooms in the early 1990s and is now moving to the blogosphere, experts and bloggers said.

A 2006 University of Maryland study on chat rooms found that female participants received 25 times as many sexually explicit and malicious messages as males. A 2005 study by the Pew Internet & American Life Project found that the proportion of Internet users who took part in chats and discussion groups plunged from 28 percent in 2000 to 17 percent in 2005, entirely because of the exodus of women. The study attributed the trend to "sensitivity to worrisome behavior in chat rooms."

Joan Walsh, editor in chief of the online magazine *Salon*, said that since the letters section of her site was automated a year and a half ago, "it's been hard to ignore that the criticisms of women writers are much more brutal and vicious than those about men."

Arianna Huffington, whose Huffington Post site is among the most prominent of blogs founded by women, said anonymity online has allowed "a lot of those dark prejudices towards women to surface." Her site takes a "zero tolerance" policy toward abusive and excessively foul language, and employs moderators "24/7" to filter the comments, she said.

Harassment Makes Women Reluctant to Blog

Sierra, whose recent case has attracted international attention, has suspended blogging. Other women have censored themselves, turned to private forums or closed comments on blogs. Many use gender-neutral pseudonyms. Some just gut it out. But the effect of repeated harassment, bloggers and exports interviewed said, is to make women reluctant to participate online—undercutting the promise of the Internet as an egalitarian forum.

Robert Scoble, a technology blogger who took a week off in solidarity with Sierra, said women have told him that harassment is a "disincentive" to participate online. That, he said, will affect their job prospects in the male-dominated tech industry. "If women aren't willing to show up for networking events, either offline or online, then they're never going to be included in the industry," he said.

The treatment of women online is not just an equivalent of what happens offline, some women say. The Internet allows the content to be seen immediately, often permanently and far more widely than a remark scribbled on a restroom wall.

"The sad thing is, I've had thousands of messages from women saying, 'You were a role model for me,'" Sierra said in an interview, describing communications she received after suspending her blog. Sierra was the first woman to deliver a keynote speech at a conference on the Linux operating system. Her blog was No. 23 in the Technorati.com Top 100 list of blogs, measured by the number of blogs that linked to her site.

Her Web site, Creating Passionate Users, was about "the most fluffy and nice things," she said. Sierra occasionally got the random "comment troll," she said, but a little over a month ago [May 2007], the posts became more threatening. Someone typed a comment on her blog about slitting her throat and ejaculating. The noose photo appeared next, on a site that sprang up to harass her. On the site, someone contributed this comment: "the only thing Kathy has to offer me is that noose in her neck size."

On yet another Web site came the muzzle photo, which struck her as if she were being smothered. "I dream of Kathy Sierra," read the caption.

Two factors can contribute to the vitriol . . .: blogging in a male-dominated field, such as technology, and achieving a degree of prominence.

"That's when I got pushed over the edge," she said. In what she intended to be her final blog post last month, she wrote: "I have cancelled all speaking engagements. I am afraid to leave my yard. I will never feel the same. I will never *be* the same."

Negativity on Blogs Is No Longer Rare

She received thousands of comments expressing outrage, including e-mails from women attesting to their own ordeals, "saying I got this. I got that. I went underground. I blogged under a pseudonym," she said.

Two factors can contribute to the vitriol, experts said: blogging in a male-dominated field, such as technology, and achieving a degree of prominence.

Susan Herring, a professor of information science at Indiana University, said each new online venue has been greeted with optimism because the early adopters tend to be educated, socially conscious people who think the form engenders community. Even as recently as 2003, she said, it was relatively rare to find negativity on blogs. Now, she said, blogs risk becoming "nastified," at least in the comment zones.

Kathleen Cooper, the single mother, said she began to experience harassment about five years ago after she posted a retort on a friend's blog to a random blogger's threat against a friend. The harasser began posting defamatory accusations on Cooper's site, on his blog and then on a site that purports to track "bad businesses." He said that he could not be responsible for what "his minions" might do to her, she said.

Cooper, 37, who lives in Sarasota, Fla., has tried password-protecting her site. She and five other women have asked the man's Web site server to shut him down, but he revives his site with another server. Law enforcement officials laugh it off, she said, "like 'Oh, it's not a big deal. It's just online talk. Nobody's going to come get you.'"

Some bloggers have called for a voluntary code of conduct, including a ban on anonymous comments.

Some Female Bloggers Are Not Intimidated

Some female bloggers say their colleagues just need thicker skin. Columnist Michelle Malkin, who blogs about politics and culture, said she sympathizes with Sierra but has chided the bloggers expressing outrage now. "First, where have y'all been? For several years, the unhinged Internet underworld has been documented here," she wrote, reposting a comment on her site that called for the "torture, rape, murder" of her family.

Report the serious threats to law enforcement, she urged. And above all: "Keep blogging. Don't cut and run."

But Herring said Malkin is in a minority. "There's a whole bunch of women who are being intimidated," she said. They include academics, professional programmers and other women normally unafraid to speak their minds.

"I completely changed," said a professor, who spoke on the condition of anonymity to avoid further harassment. "I self-censor like crazy because I don't feel like getting caught up in another round of abuse."

Some bloggers have called for a voluntary code of conduct, including a ban on anonymous comments. But other bloggers resist because it seems like a restriction of free speech. The founders of BlogHer, a 10,000-member online community supporting women, said the best way to enforce civility on a blog is for each site to create its own rules—such as removing abusive comments—then make the rules public and apply them fairly.

Herring said the decline in women's participation in chat rooms was ominous. "If we see a lot of harassment in the blogosphere, will we see a decline in women blogging? I think we will."

Blogging May Lead to a Change in Libel Laws

Laura Parker

Laura Parker is a staff writer at USA Today.

Rafe Banks, a lawyer in Georgia, got involved in a nasty dispute with a client over how to defend him on a drunken-driving charge. The client, David Milum, fired Banks and demanded that the lawyer refund a $3,000 fee. Banks refused.

Milum eventually was acquitted. Ordinarily, that might have been the last Banks ever heard about his former client. But then Milum started a blog.

In May 2004, Banks was stunned to learn that Milum's blog was accusing the lawyer of bribing judges on behalf of drug dealers. At the end of one posting, Milum wrote: "Rafe, don't you wish you had given back my $3,000 retainer?"

Blogs ... increasingly are being targeted by those who feel harmed by blog attacks.

Banks, saying the postings were false, sued Milum. And last January [2006], Milum became the first blogger in the USA to lose a libel suit, according to the Media Law Resource Center in New York, which tracks litigation involving bloggers. Milum was ordered to pay Banks $50,000.

The case reflected how blogs—short for web logs, the burgeoning, freewheeling Internet forums that give people the power to instantly disseminate messages worldwide—increasingly are being targeted by those who feel harmed by blog attacks. In the past two years [2004–2006], more than 50 lawsuits stemming from postings on blogs and website message boards have been filed across the nation. The suits have spawned a debate over how the "blogosphere" and its revolutionary impact on speech and publishing might change libel law.

Lawsuits Are Aimed at Silencing Attackers

Legal analysts say the lawsuits are challenging a mind-set that has long surrounded blogging: that most bloggers essentially are "judgment-proof" because they—unlike traditional media such as newspapers, magazines and television outlets—often are ordinary citizens who don't have a lot of money. Recent lawsuits by Banks and others who say they have had their reputations harmed or their privacy violated have been aimed not just at cash awards but also at silencing their critics.

> *The blogosphere . . . is the Internet's Wild West, a rapidly expanding frontier town with no sheriff.*

"Bloggers didn't think they could be subject to libel," says Eric Robinson, a Media Law Resource Center attorney. "You take what is on your mind, type it and post it."

The legal battles over blogging and message board postings are unfolding on several fronts:

- In Washington, D.C., former U.S. Senate aide Jessica Cutler was sued for invasion of privacy by Robert Steinbuch, also a former Senate aide, after Cutler posted a blog in 2004 describing their sexual escapades. The blog, titled *Washingtonienne*, was viewed widely after it was cited by a Washington gossip website called Wonkette. [Later], Steinbuch added Wonkette to the lawsuit.

- Todd Hollis, a criminal defense lawyer in Pittsburgh, has filed a libel suit against a website called DontDate

HimGirl.com, which includes message boards in which women gossip about men they supposedly dated. One posting on the site accused Hollis of having herpes. Another said he had infected a woman he once dated with a sexually transmitted disease. Yet another said he was gay. Hollis, 38, who says the accusations are false, is suing the site's operator, Tasha Joseph, and the posters of the messages.

- Anna Draker, a high school assistant principal in San Antonio, filed a defamation and negligence lawsuit against two students and their parents after a hoax page bearing her name, photo and several lewd comments and graphics appeared on MySpace.com, the popular social networking website. The suit alleges that the students—one of whom had been disciplined by Draker—created the page to get revenge, and that it was designed to "injure Ms.Draker's reputation, expose her to public hatred . . . and cause her harm." The suit also alleges that the youths' parents were grossly negligent in supervising them.

- Ligonier Ministries, a religious broadcaster and publisher in Lake Mary, Fla., has taken the unusual step of asking a judge to preemptively silence a blogger to try to prevent him from criticizing the ministries. Judges historically have refused to place such limits on traditional publishers. The lawsuit cites postings on a blog by Frank Vance that described Ligonier president Timothy Dick as "a shark" and as coming from a "family of nincompoops." The suit says the entries are false and have damaged Dick's reputation.

Robert Cox, founder and president of the Media Bloggers Association, which has 1,000 members, says the recent wave of lawsuits means that bloggers should bone up on libel law. "It hasn't happened yet, but soon, there will be a blogger who is successfully sued and who loses his home," he says. "That will be the shot heard round the blogosphere."

Wild West of the Internet

At its best, the blogosphere represents the ultimate in free speech by giving voice to millions. It is the Internet's version of Speaker's Corner in London's Hyde Park, a global coffeehouse where ideas are debated and exchanged.

People take advantage of the anonymity to say things in public they would never say to anyone face-to-face.

The blogosphere also is the Internet's Wild West, a rapidly expanding frontier town with no sheriff. It's a place where both truth and "truthiness" thrive, to use the satirical word coined by comedian Stephen Colbert as a jab at politicians for whom facts don't matter.

Nearly two blogs are created every second, according to Technorati, a San Francisco firm that tracks more than 53 million blogs. Besides forming online communities in which people share ideas, news and gossip and debate issues of the day, blogs empower character assassins and mischief makers.

Small disputes now can lead to huge embarrassment, thanks to websites such as bitterwaitress.com, which purports to identify restaurant patrons who leave miserly tips. Dont DateHimGirl.com includes postings that have identified men as pedophiles, rapists and diseased, without verification the postings are true.

The chief danger in legal disputes over what's said on the Internet is the potential chilling effect it could have on free speech.

"People take advantage of the anonymity to say things in public they would never say to anyone face-to-face," Cox says.

"That's where you get these horrible comments. This is standard operating procedure."

Even so, Cox thinks the chief danger in legal disputes over what's said on the Internet is the potential chilling effect it could have on free speech. Many lawsuits against bloggers, he says, are filed merely to silence critics. In those cases, he encourages bloggers to fight back.

Last April [2006], Cox orchestrated an effective counterattack on behalf of a blogger in Maine who was sued by a New York ad agency for $1 million. Lance Dutson, a website designer, had been blogging for two years when he posted several essays accusing Maine's Department of Tourism of wasting taxpayers' money. Among other things, he posted a draft of a tourism ad that mistakenly had contained a toll-free number to a phone-sex line.

Warren Kremer Paino Advertising [WKPA], which produced the tourism campaign, said in its suit that Dutson made defamatory statements "designed to blacken WKPA's reputation (and) expose WKPA to public contempt and ridicule."

Dutson's criticisms paled to those directed at WKPA after word of the lawsuit spread through the blogosphere. Bloggers rushed to defend Dutson, and several lawyers volunteered to represent him. The media picked up the story and cast it as David vs. Goliath. Eight days after filing the suit, WKPA dropped it without comment.

"We're not here to play nice with somebody who is trying to suppress the speech of one of my members," Cox says.

Who Should Be Sued?

A key principle that courts use in determining whether someone has been libeled is what damage the offending article did to that person's reputation in his or her community.

Susan Crawford, a professor at Cardoza Law School in New York who specializes in media and Internet issues, says the ease with which false postings can be corrected instantly, among other things, will force judges to reconsider how to measure the damage that is done to a plaintiff's reputation.

"Libel law depends on having a reputation in a particular town that's damaged," she says. "Do you have an online reputation? What's your community that hears about the damage to your online reputation? Who should be sued? The original poster? Or someone like the Wonkette, for making something really famous? The causes of action won't go away. But judges will be skeptical that a single, four-line (posting in a) blog has actually damaged anyone."

Greg Herbert, an Orlando lawyer who represented Dutson, disagrees. The principles of libel law aren't going to change, he says. However, some judges "might not think a blogger is entitled to the same sort of free speech protection others are. A lot of judges still don't know what a blog is, and they think the Internet is a dark and nefarious place where all kinds of evil deeds occur."

Judges have indicated that they will give wide latitude to the type of speech being posted on the Internet. They usually have cited the 1996 Communications Decency Act, which protects website owners from being held liable for postings by others. On the other hand, under that statute, individuals who post messages are responsible for their content and can be sued for libel. That applies whether they are posting on their own website or on others' message boards.

In May [2006], a federal judge in Philadelphia cited the act in dismissing a lawsuit stemming from a series of postings on a website operated by Tucker Max, a Duke Law School graduate whose site features tales of his boozing and womanizing.

Posters on a message board on tuckermax.com had ridiculed Anthony DiMeo III, the heir to a New Jersey blueberry farm fortune, accusing him of inflating his credentials as a publicist, event planner and actor. DiMeo sued Max last

March, claiming in court papers that his manhood had been questioned, his professional skills lampooned and his social connections mocked. DiMeo said Max, through the website, had libeled and threatened him, noting that one poster had written: "I can't believe no one has killed (DiMeo) yet."

In dismissing the suit, U.S. District Judge Steward Daizell noted that Max "could be a poster child for the vulgarity" on the Internet, but that he nevertheless was entitled to protection under the Communications Decency Act. After the decision, DiMeo ridiculers on tuckermax.com piled on. Max says more than 200,000 people have viewed various threads on his message board about DiMeo.

DiMeo has asked an appeals court to consider not only the original messages about him but also those posted since the court decision. Alan Nochumson, DiMeo's attorney, says the criticism has amounted to an Internet gang attack, led by Max, that has significantly damaged DiMeo's business. Nochumson says when Internet users use Google to search for DiMeo's name, many of the first web links that pop up direct readers to postings on Max's website that criticize DiMeo.

Max says the claim is absurd. "The Internet isn't some giant ant colony," he says. "Different people from all over the country do things. I don't control them."

Third-Party Comments

Hollis' lawsuit against DontDateHimGirl.com could reveal how far courts are willing to go to protect website owners from third-party comments. His suit claims the site is not the equivalent of an Internet provider such as AOL or Yahoo, and that because Joseph edits the site, she should be liable for its contents.

Hollis has sued Joseph, a Miami publicist and former *Miami Herald* columnist, as well as seven women who posted the messages about him. Three are named in the suit; four are anonymous.

Joseph's attorney, Lida Rodriguez-Taseff, says Joseph does not edit postings, except to remove information such as Social Security numbers and addresses.

"If a court were to find that the Communications Decency Act doesn't apply to Tasha, no website would be safe," Rodriguez-Taseff says, adding that if courts start to hold website owners liable for the content of third-party postings, "the only people who would be able to provide forums (would be) wealthy people. . . . It would be like making the coffee shop owner responsible for what people say in his coffee shop. What this case would say is that providers of forums in the Internet would have an obligation to determine truth or falsity of posts.". . .

"The Internet has a great number of valuable tools with which people can do great things," Hollis says.

But he says he's disturbed by how such false personal information can spread so freely across the web. "Even if I had herpes, which I don't, even if I was gay, which I'm not, would I want to have a conversation about those things with an anonymous individual over a global platform? It's utterly ridiculous."

Even if he wins in court, Hollis says, he loses. "Those postings are going to be out there forever," he says. "Whenever anybody Googles my name, up comes a billion sites. I will forever have to explain to someone that I do not have herpes."

Basic Defense for Libel: The Truth

In Cumming, Ga., about 40 miles northeast of Atlanta, David Milum, 58, is still blogging. He is appealing the $50,000 judgment against him.

Milum says he considers himself a muckraker and exposer of corruption in local officials. In the recent libel trial, his attorney, Jeff Butler, described his client as a "rabble-rouser" whose inspiration was "public service."

Milum lost in court because he could not meet the basic defense for libel claims: He could not prove that his allegations that Banks was involved in bribery and corruption were true. Now Milum is facing another libel suit—this one seeking $2 million—over his claims about the alleged misdeeds of a local government employee.

"I have a very wonderful wife," Milum says. "And you can imagine how wonderful she has to be to put up with this."

Free Speech in Blogs May Be Restricted by Employers

Jonathan A. Segal

Jonathan A. Segal is a contributing editor of HR Magazine *and a partner in a Philadelphia employment services group.*

Diane is a stellar employee who works very hard during the day; she loves to blog at night. That is, she has created a web log—"blog"—in which she airs her strong political views.

Greg also is an excellent employee. He too blogs at night, not expressing political opinions, but rather venting frustration with his employer's policies and practices.

Sally rounds out the blogging trio. She just wants to have fun. Her blogging is limited to concocting sexual fantasies so explicit they would make even "Sex and the City" character Samantha Jones blush.

Private employers can proscribe or punish blogging without violating their employees' First Amendment rights. In contrast, public employers must take First Amendment restrictions into account.

The CEO calls you into her office and tells you that she wants you to fire all three bloggers. She disagrees with Diane's politics and fears a major customer will, too. She is upset that Greg has publicly aired the employer's dirty laundry. She believes that Sally's blogging is an embarrassment to the company, particularly since Sally is visible to the public as a recruiter.

Can you legally fire any or all of them? Should you fire any or all of them? What about imposing restrictions on off-duty blogging for all employees going forward?

To help you answer these questions, this article surveys the legal landscape surrounding off-duty blogging, examines other consequences of cracking down on off-duty blogging and suggests a case-by-case approach to dealing with off-duty blogging that takes all these issues into account.

Of course, the rules are different when it comes to on-duty blogging. In that case, an employer's rights are greater, particularly if the employee is using the employer's technology. However, that does not necessarily mean that employers need to have a policy specific to on-duty blogging. To avoid developing new policies for every technological change, employers are well advised to draft their technology-use policies broadly enough to anticipate and cover innovations—without addressing each and every one of them separately.

Legal Landscape

Our analysis begins with the employment-at-will principle. As we all know from the oh-so-welcoming disclaimers in our employee handbooks, an employer can discharge an at-will employee at any time, for any reason, no reason, a good reason or a bad reason—just not an illegal reason. So, we start with the premise that an employer acts lawfully when it considers off-duty conduct in making an adverse employment decision.

Like all legal generalities, however, the at-will rule is subject to exceptions. Employers need to scrutinize carefully the legality of any adverse action based on off-duty blogging (or any other off-duty speech) in light of various exceptions.

Free speech rights. Employees may argue that firing them for blogging violates their First Amendment right to freedom of speech. A surprise to many employees, however, is that the

First Amendment to the federal Constitution limits only governmental action; it does not restrict private employers' behavior.

Accordingly, private employers can proscribe or punish blogging without violating their employees' First Amendment rights. In contrast, public employers must take First Amendment restrictions into account.

Some state constitutions—California's, for example—apply to public and private employers alike. So employers in those states need to consider the state's constitutional equivalent to the First Amendment in assessing employee rights.

Off-duty protection statutes. Employees without constitutional protection nevertheless may be covered by broad off-duty protection statutes that may encompass off-duty blogging. A number of states—New York and Colorado among them—have enacted such laws.

Saying that an action is not unlawful does not mean that it is without legal implications.

The New York statute, for example, prohibits an employer from taking adverse action against an employee for off-duty political activities, union activities, legal use of consumable products and recreational activities. The term "recreational activities" is defined relatively broadly to include "sports, games, hobbies, exercise, reading, and viewing of television, movies and similar materials." For some, blogging undeniably is a hobby.

In New York, at least, all three of our bloggers might be protected. At a minimum, there would be an issue to litigate as to whether the employee's blogging rises to the level of a hobby or other recreational activity.

A number of other states—Missouri and Nevada are two—have narrower statutes that protect political expression exclusively. The Missouri law, for example, makes it unlawful for an employer to prevent or attempt to prevent an employee from engaging in political activities.

While Diane might be protected by political expression statutes in some states, Sally and Greg would not. They are not political bloggers. But apolitical blogging very easily could morph into political blogging. For example, Greg's blogging could become protected as political if he advocated legislation to prevent other employers from engaging in the employment practices he is complaining about.

Civil Rights Act Provisions

Anti-retaliation provisions. Employers also need to consider the anti-retaliation provisions of federal and state laws that prohibit job discrimination or otherwise regulate the employment relationship. Title VII of the Civil Rights Act of 1964, for example, prohibits an employer from retaliating against an employee because he or she has "opposed" any unlawful practice. . . .

In terms of Title VII retaliation, Greg is the only blogger likely to enjoy protection—and that would depend on the underlying reasons for his dissatisfaction. If Greg complains that all employees are paid too little, he probably is not protected by Title VII. But if he blogs that only male employees are paid too little, he may be protected by Title VII, which prohibits sex discrimination.

Protected concerted activity. Even if Greg is not a member of a union, he may be protected under the National Labor Relations Act if he is blogging about terms and conditions of employment that affect not only him but also his co-workers. In other words, as long as Greg does not focus exclusively on his own grievances, he may be engaged in protected concerted activity when grousing publicly about terms and conditions of employment. . . .

Whistle-blower protections. What if Greg is complaining not about how the company treats employees, but about how it treats its shareholders? Suppose he alleges that the employer is cooking the books in violation of the Sarbanes-Oxley Act?

Even if an employee's off-duty blogging is not protected by a federal or state statute, it may be protected by a state's common law, as reflected in its judicial opinions.

Sarbanes-Oxley includes a very broad whistle-blower provision, but it may not cover whistle-blowing bloggers. By its express terms, the anti-retaliation provision covers only complaints made to certain entities or individuals:

- A federal regulatory or law enforcement agency.

- Any member or committee of Congress.

- A person who holds supervisory authority over the employee or has authority to investigate, discover or terminate misconduct.

Sarbanes-Oxley does not appear to cover complaints made to the world at large.

Where an employer has, or probably has, the right to regulate an employee's off-duty blogging, that does not mean that the employer should do so.

But saying that an action is not unlawful does not mean that it is without legal implications. While terminating an off-duty whistle-blowing blogger probably does not amount to unlawful retaliation under Sarbanes-Oxley, it may very well raise negative implications before the investigating commission, a judge or a jury. Plus, it would have the media salivating. The bottom line is that employers cannot generalize relative to whistle-blowing bloggers. We must examine the specific statute upon which the whistle-blower relies.

Public policy protection. Even if an employee's off-duty blogging is not protected by a federal or state statute, it may be protected by a state's common law, as reflected in its judicial opinions. In most states, there is a public policy exception to the at-will principle that at least arguably could be applied to off-duty speech.

Contractual rights. Finally, an individual employment agreement or a collective bargaining agreement may limit an employer's freedom to consider off-duty conduct. In other words, if the employee is not at-will, the employer's freedom to terminate is restricted.

Many executive employment agreements provide that an employee cannot be terminated except for "cause" during a stated period. Alternatively, such agreements often call for severance if the employee is terminated without cause. Virtually all union contracts require "just cause" for non-probationary employees, who can challenge their discharge before an arbitrator.

Prohibiting or punishing blogging should not constitute a legal invasion of privacy because blogging, by definition, is public in nature.

So the question becomes whether and when off-duty conduct can establish the requisite "cause" or "just cause" for termination or for withholding severance. We begin here with the presumption there is no cause or no just cause unless the employer can establish a clear nexus between the employee's off-duty conduct and the employer's reputation, profitability or mission.

With respect to all three of our blogging cases, the CEO has articulated a workplace connection. More facts are needed to predict whether an arbitrator would find it adequate to justify termination.

An arbitrator probably would consider whether an employee names the employer in the blog. Even without an explicit reference, other facts might make it possible for readers to identify the company on their own. In that case, an arbitrator might conclude that including the employer's name is not necessary to make the connection.

Arbitrators also are likely to consider whether the employer gave employees advance notice of restrictions on off-duty blogging. Arbitrators are mindful of due process, and there is no reason to believe that they would ignore the issue of notice when it comes to blogging.

Finally, arbitrators almost always consider an employee's entire record, including tenure, job performance and other disciplinary issues.

Employees are likely to perceive discipline or termination of an employee for off-duty blogging as employer over-reaching.

Consciously or unconsciously, judges and juries may consider the same factors as an arbitrator in deciding any other claim challenging an employer's regulation of off-duty blogging. Legal niceties aside, fairness always matters.

Might Makes . . . Right?

Where an employer has, or probably has, the right to regulate an employee's off-duty blogging, that does not mean that the employer should do so. An I-can-so-I-will style of management creates other risks that employers need to take into account.

As always, there are employee relations considerations. Employees that do not blog still may fear: What's next? Will the employer regulate what I read? What I say at dinner?

Prohibiting or punishing blogging should not constitute a legal invasion of privacy because blogging, by definition, is public in nature. Nevertheless, perceptions are important in the realm of employee relations.

In the absence of a compelling employer interest, employees are likely to perceive discipline or termination of an employee for off-duty blogging as employer overreaching. It may even prompt some employees to leave the company. Those without that option may try to restrict management's right to flex its legal muscles through collective action—in other words, unionization. The old adage "Police yourself or be policed" is particularly apt to employer regulation of off-duty conduct.

There also is the question of your customers. If an employer is seen as demonizing certain conduct, "demons" outside the workplace are less likely to want to do business with you. By discharging an employee for political expression, you may risk alienating a substantial percentage of your customers and potential customers.

Then there is a practical concern: Terminating bloggers may result in more damage than retaining them in your control. Bloggers have a lot of passion. Do you really want to give them free time, too? If you are worried about an employee's blogging, imagine what he might say when he has lots of time and anger and nothing to lose!

Balancing Act

When we take all of the above considerations into account, there is not always a clear answer as to what an employer should do in response to an instance of off-duty blogging. Rather, the decision-making process usually involves a balancing of complex—and sometimes competing—legal and business considerations that may turn on the content of the blog, the employee's position with the organization and, of course, the state in which the employee blogs.

To ensure greater certainty, some blogging rights advocates and management attorneys have called upon employers to develop policies notifying bloggers of what they can and cannot do. . . .

But the array of legal and practical issues that employers need to consider in deciding how to respond to specific instances of blogging also apply to whether to have a blogging policy.

Adopting an off-duty blogging policy may have similar or worse employee relations consequences than disciplining a particular blogger. Even employees who don't really understand or care about blogging may be fearful of their employer playing Big Brother.

There are also complex legal issues employers would need to consider in developing a policy on off-duty blogging. To ensure that any such policy is not overbroad, the employer arguably should carve out "protected" blogging. Do you really want to say, "You can't grouse generally about your job, but you can grouse specifically about discrimination"?

And, if we are going to develop a blogging policy, why not a policy restricting the messages employees sport on T-shirts, hats and bumper stickers? Do you want an employee who is publicly associated with your organization to wear a "smoke dope" T-shirt while walking through the mall? Of course not, but you do not need a policy to address it.

Not every issue requires a policy. Instead, sometimes a general statement of the employer's expectations that has potentially broad application is sufficient. For example, "We expect all employees to act professionally on the job, and to refrain from behavior, on and off the job, that could adversely impact the employer's reputation or mission."

An employer could rely on this kind of general statement of expectations to deal with problematic off-duty bloggers as well as with other problematic off-duty conduct without running the risk that every employee will want to read or re-read *1984,* George Orwell's dystopian classic that gave birth to Big Brother.

Students Have the Right to Blog

Electronic Frontier Foundation

The Electronic Frontier Foundation is a donor-funded nonprofit organization that champions citizens' freedom online, primarily by bringing and defending lawsuits.

Do public school students have free speech rights under the First Amendment?

Absolutely. Both minors and adults have First Amendment rights, and according to the Supreme Court, public school students don't "shed their constitutional right to freedom of speech or expression at the schoolhouse gate." See *Tinker v. Des Moines Independent Community School District*, 393 U.S. 503 (1969). In the *Tinker* case, the Court said that public high school students had a First Amendment right to wear black armbands to class in symbolic protest of the Vietnam War. "Students in school as well as out of school are 'persons' under our Constitution," the Court said, and "they are possessed of fundamental rights which the State must respect ..."

But I'm a private school student—what about me?

You also have First Amendment rights, but those rights only protect you from government censorship, not private censorship. As a general matter, you will receive no protection from censorship or punishment by a private school or college. See e.g. *Ubriaco v. Albertus Magnus High School*, No. 99 Civ. 11135 (JSM) (S.D.N.Y. July 21, 2000) (dismissing claim contesting private school expulsion for content on personal web site). However, ... some states provide private high school and college students with additional speech protections that

Electronic Frontier Foundation, "Bloggers' FAQ on Student Blogging," www.eff.org, August 21, 2007. Reproduced by permission.

go above and beyond the First Amendment. Furthermore, if your private school has an applicable written policy, the school must follow that policy. . . .

Can public schools censor or punish students' on-campus speech?

Yes, whether you're a minor or an adult, in high school or in college. Although the *Tinker* decision recognized that students have free speech rights on campus, the court also held that your free-speech rights can be limited when the speech "materially disrupts classwork or involves substantial disorder or invasion of the rights of others." This rule is referred to as *Tinker*'s "material disruption" standard, or the *Tinker* test. For example, a school can "prohibit the use of vulgar and offensive terms in public discourse" while you are on campus *Bethel School District No. 403 v. Fraser,* 478 U.S. 675 (1986) (upholding suspension of a high-school student Matthew Fraser for a student government nomination speech "including the use of obscene, profane language or gestures.").

Can public high school administrators censor what I say in a school-hosted blog or other school-sponsored publication?

Usually, but it depends on the facts. In *Hazelwood Sch. Dist. v. Kuhlmeier,* 484 U.S. 260 (1988), the Supreme Court distinguished a school-sponsored newspaper from the armbands permitted in *Tinker* and allowed censorship that was "reasonably related to legitimate pedagogical concerns." This rule is referred to as the *Hazelwood* standard or the *Hazelwood* test. The *Hazelwood* standard applies to censorship of "school-sponsored publications, theatrical productions, and other expressive activities that students, parents, and members of the public might reasonably perceive to bear the imprimatur of the school." "Imprimatur of the school" refers to activities that appear to be sponsored or endorsed by the school.

The *Hazelwood* standard is less protective of your rights than the *Tinker* test. However, there is one bright spot: the *Hazelwood* standard does not apply to publications that have been opened as "public forums for student expression," even if those publications are school-sponsored.

Some lower courts have applied the Tinker *"material disruption" standard in cases concerning the personal web sites of high school and middle school students.*

Is my school-hosted blog a public forum?

A public forum is one where the student bloggers, not school administrators, have the authority to determine the content. Whether a school-hosted blog would be considered a public forum, and therefore not subject to *Hazelwood* censorship, is determined on a case-by-case basis, looking at the school's policies and statements. If your school has an Internet Policy or Terms of Use for its site-hosting services, look it over carefully to see if the school has a right to edit or censor content.

Don't post anything that someone at school is likely to take as a direct physical threat against school staff or students.

Can public college administrators censor my school-hosted blog?

Probably not, unless justified under *Tinker*'s "material disruption" test as described above. Courts have generally found that the protective *Hazelwood* standard (that allows school censorship) only applies to high schools, and censorship of a student's publication by a public college or university would amount to an unconstitutional prior restraint. . . .

But wait, these cases are about student newspapers, not blogs!

Yes. In the U.S. legal system, it generally takes a while for the courts to reach decisions that clarify how the law will be applied to new technologies or mediums of expression, like blogs. However, if there were a lawsuit, your attorney could argue by analogy, showing the court how blogging is similar to traditional media, and should have the same protections.

Do I have more protections for a personal blog?

Yes. In *Emmett v. Kent School District,* 92 F. Supp.2d 1088 (W.D. Wash. 2000), the court held that public school officials had violated a student's First Amendment rights by punishing the student for his personal website, the "Unofficial Kentlake High Home Page." The court held that "[a]lthough the intended audience was undoubtedly connected to Kentlake High School, the speech was entirely outside of the school's supervision or control." Likewise, in *Flaherty v. Keystone Oaks School Dist.,* 247 F.Supp.2d 698 (W.D. Pa. 2003) a federal court found a public school's policy, which prohibited "inappropriate, harassing, offensive or abusive" behavior, was unconstitutional because "the policy could be (and is) read by school officials to cover speech that occurs off school premises and that is not related to any school activity in an arbitrary manner."

Sweet, my personal blog is untouchable!

Not so fast. EFF [the Electronic Frontier Foundation] believes that public schools have no right to punish or censor any speech activities conducted outside of the school gates, and the Supreme Court has yet to consider such off-campus censorship. However, some lower courts have applied the *Tinker* "material disruption" standard in cases concerning the personal web sites of high school and middle school students. For example, in *Beussink v. Woodland School District,* 30 F. Supp.2d 1175 (E.D. Mo.1998), a federal court applied *Tinker's* "material disruption" standard when considering a student's web site that used vulgar language to criticize his public school and its teachers and administrators. Even though the site was created on the student's own time, with his own computer and Internet connection, the court decided that the *Tinker* "material disruption" test applied since a classmate viewed the site at school. While it is unfortunate that the court applied the less protective standard, in the end the student was vindicated—since there was no material disruption, the court decided that the student's First Amendment rights were violated.

Likewise, in *J.S. ex rel H.S. v. Bethlehem Area School District,* 569 A.2d 638 (Pa. 2002), the Supreme Court of Pennsylvania held that despite the fact that the web site was not created at school, the *Tinker* test applied because the site "was aimed at a specific school and/or its personnel" and was "brought onto the school campus or accessed at school by its originator." The court proceeded to hold that the public school's punishment of a student for his off-campus web site, which included an image of a teacher's face morphing into Hitler's, an image of the same teacher with a decapitated head dripping with blood, and a request that visitors contribute $20 for a hit man, was justified under the "material disruption" standard. . . .

Just as you have First Amendment rights like other bloggers, you're also subject to all the same legal responsibilities.

So can I criticize teachers on my blog?

It depends on how you do it. Merely criticizing or insulting schoolteachers and administrators, even with vulgar language, likely will not amount to the "material disruption" required by the Supreme Court. . . .

However, if you publish anything that might be considered a physical threat toward a student, teacher, or administrator, a court will likely find that punishment by the school is constitutional. . . .

Similarly, although your opinions are protected by the First Amendment, publishing defamatory content . . .—even jokingly—may get you in trouble at school, and maybe even get you sued. Other types of speech may also violate the law and put you within reach of the school's discipline . . .

Can I publish sexual content on my blog?

Yes, as long as it's not obscene. However, it's important to note that obscenity law applies differently to minors and adults. In *Ginsberg v. New York*, 390 U.S. 629, the Supreme Court found a lower standard of obscenity applies when the speech is directed toward minors: speech is obscene as to minors (or "harmful to minors") if it (1) appeals to the prurient, shameful, or morbid interest of minors, (2) is patently offensive to prevailing standards in the adult community as a whole with respect to what is suitable for minors, and (3) is utterly without redeeming social importance for minors. . . .

However, you do have a clear constitutional right to post explicit sexual content that isn't just meant to be arousing, but is related to social issues like sexual health that are important to minors.

Don't encourage other students to read or post comments to your blog while at school.

What can I do to avoid causing a "material disruption" at school with my personal blog?

Based on how the courts have applied the "material disruption" standard to off-campus web sites in the past, there are several things you can do to avoid a situation where the school might discipline you:

- Most importantly, don't post anything that someone at school is likely to take as a direct physical threat against school staff or students.

- Don't advocate for the immediate violation of any laws or school rules. . . .

- Make sure you aren't publishing anything illegal. Just as you have First Amendment rights like other bloggers, you're also subject to all the same legal responsibilities.

- Don't use any school resources to publish or view your blog.

- Don't encourage other students to read or post comments to your blog while at school—tell them to wait until they are off campus. If you see comments on your blog posted by other students during school hours, consider deleting them.

- Make sure it's clear to readers that the blog isn't sponsored by or affiliated with the school.

- Before you start cussing or bagging on people, take a second to cool off. Although we think you have a right to use coarse language to describe people at school, and several courts have agreed with us, it will still increase the chance that your school will try to punish you.

While you can change your blog post at any time, it may be archived by others.

What if I want to advocate civil disobedience on my blog?

If you want to, for example, call for a student walk-out or otherwise advocate for civil disobedience that might be considered a "material disruption" at school, or if you just want to be able to freely criticize teachers and students without fear of getting unjustly punished, you should blog anonymously.

Even if you're blogging anonymously, though, you still shouldn't publish anything illegal—first off, you don't want to break the law, and second, publishing illegal material will increase the chance that someone will try to subpoena your Internet Service Provider or your blog host for your real identity. . . .

Do I have a first amendment right to blog anonymously?

Yes. You have a first Amendment right to speak anonymously (both online and elsewhere) and to protect your identity from subpoenas. . . .

What if I get punished for my personal blog?

Contact your lawyer. . . . Even those courts that have used the "material disruption" test when evaluating school punishments for off-campus web sites have usually found the punishments to be unconstitutional. In fact, some students who have been punished for their personal web sites have been able to get their school records cleared and obtain cash settlements from their schools in exchange for dropping or not bringing a lawsuit. . . .

Most schools, when faced with the threat of a suit for a clearly unconstitutional punishment, will back down and clear your record.

Can I republish rumors on my blog?

Not if it is false and will cause harm to someone's reputation. If you blog based on a rumor that the dude in the back row of chemistry class is a pothead, or that the head cheerleader has hooked up with half the football team, or that the principal is having an affair with the algebra teacher, and it ends up not being true, then you may have defamed those people. . . .

Should I blog about my fellow students' private lives?

Not without asking. People can get upset if you spread their secrets. Ask friends and family what types of stuff they're comfortable with you sharing on your blog. When you take pictures for your online photo album, be considerate and ask your subjects if they don't mind before you post it.

OK, so maybe it's uncool, but is it illegal to blog about someone's private business?

Outing a friend who told you about things like a private medical condition or family problem is not only really lame, it also could violate "publication of private facts" law, which is designed to protect a person's private information even if the information is truthful. . . .

Although a school has little power to punish you for off-campus speech, it can still use your blog against you as evidence of other rules violations.

What about blogging about my own private life?

Keep in mind that whatever you post on a public blog can be seen by your friends, your enemies, your teachers, your parents, your ex, that Great Aunt who likes to pinch your cheeks like you're a baby, the admissions offices of schools and colleges to which you might apply, current and future potential employers, and anyone else with access to the Internet and a search engine. While you can change your blog post at any time, it may be archived by others.

So, before you reveal personal information online, carefully consider whether you want that to be public now and in the future. And keep in mind that although a school has little power to punish you for off-campus speech, it can still use your blog against you as evidence of other rules violations. For example, several underage college students were recently punished for violating their school's alcohol policy after they posted pictures of themselves drinking.

What can I do to blog more privately?

You can use password-protected blogs and other technologies that allow a more limited audience, such as "friends-only" posts. If you don't want to blog anonymously, consider blogging under only your first name, or for even more privacy, a pseudonym. This will make it harder for people to search on your name (depending, of course, on how rare your name is). You can also use a robots.txt file to stop search engines from indexing blog pages you don't want crawled.

Blogs Can Be Used as Evidence in Court Cases

Chris W. McCarty

Chris W. McCarty is an attorney who practices in Knoxville, Tennessee.

Jury members take their seats. Just before a short recess, your opponent finished her direct examination of the defendant. This case involves an auto-accident, a classic he said, she said situation. The defendant ran a red-light, yet denied it on direct [examination].

Standing up to cross [examine] you look down for one last read. In one hand, you hold a printout of a statement the defendant made a few days after the wreck: "It was my fault, I ran a red-light."

The catch? You pulled that quote from the defendant's MySpace blog.

Blog Nation

In the case of *In re Ramon Stevens*, the California Court of Appeals defined "blog" as "[a] Web site (or section of a Web site) where users can post a chronological, up-to-date e-journal entry of their thoughts." When attempting to describe what exactly a blog might offer potential users, the popular blogging service *Blogger* offers a more expansive definition:

> A blog is a personal diary. A daily pulpit. A collaborative space. A political soapbox. A breaking-news outlet. A collection of links. Your own private thoughts. Memos to the world.

Blogs not only tell us what their authors do; they also tell us what their authors think. And those thoughts can be as random as the people responsible for them.

Although we are not always sure what to make of blogs, we do know they are multiplying. According to recent statistics, a new blog comes online every second of every day. Further, blogs both new and old produce an average of 50,000 new posts every hour.

To the world, blogs illustrate a growing movement from the private to the public. Where once teenage girls poured their hearts into leather-bound diaries, they now splash them across MySpace pages in big, pink letters.

A claim to privacy is unavailable to someone who places information on an indisputably public medium, such as the Internet, without taking any measures to protect the information.

To lawyers, on the other hand, blogs represent a source of largely underutilized information.

Public Invitation

Obviously, blogs often contain personal information. This is the type of information that, in normal circumstances, would lead lawyers head-on into privacy issues. So far, however, courts have remained clear that the Internet is not a private forum, but a public one.

For example, in *United States v. Gines-Perez*, a 2002 opinion out of the U.S. District Court for the District of Puerto Rico, Judge Daniel Dominguez remained "convinced that placing information on the information superhighway necessarily makes said matter accessible to the public[.]" After noting the lack of clear precedent to support his opinion, Judge Dominguez still found it "obvious that a claim to privacy is unavailable to someone who places information on an indisputably, public medium, such as the Internet, without taking any measures to protect the information."

In *Guest v. Leis*, a 2001 Sixth Circuit opinion, Judge Alan Norris offered similar sentiments regarding privacy and the Internet. During an online obscenity investigation, authorities seized two computer bulletin board systems. In responding to bulletin board members' allegations that said seizures violated the Fourth Amendment, Judge Norris dismissed their arguments by noting that "[u]sers would logically lack a legitimate expectation of privacy in the materials intended for publication or public posting."

By applying current case law to your car wreck defendant, it is clear that her MySpace blog is just as much your space as it is hers.

Hard Evidence

Perhaps the most public, and controversial, use of blog evidence in civil litigation involves *Washingtonienne*, a blog written by former United States Senate assistant Jessica Cutler. In *Steinbuch v. Cutler*, a 2006 case from the United States District Court for the District of Columbia, plaintiff Robert Steinbuch sued Cutler for invasion of privacy and intentional infliction of emotional distress after *Washingtonienne* posted entries "detailing [their] social and sexual activities[.]" After a recent amended complaint added co-defendant Ana Marie Cox, author of the widely popular blog *Wonkette*, the case remains ongoing and promises to offer great insight not only into the dalliances of Washington elite, but also into modern jurors' readiness to hear and evaluate blog-based evidence.

Outside of defamation and invasion of privacy suits, we are hard pressed to find civil litigators harnessing the Internet with any degree of success. For example, in *Nicholson v. City of Chattanooga*, a 2005 civil rights case from the U.S. District Court for the Eastern District of Tennessee, the plaintiff garnered very little weight with "an unidentified and unauthenticated document purporting to be an internet 'web blog[.]'" Judge R. Allan Edgar noted that the blog "purport[ed] to be ... written by one of the emergency medical professionals sent to the scene of the shooting" at issue. However, although the information cited may have appeared useful, Judge Edgar immediately diffused any usefulness by questioning the blog's origin and author.

As *Nicholson* seems to illustrate, the key question is not *if* lawyers should introduce blog-based evidence, but *how* lawyers should introduce blog-based evidence.

Careful Introduction

One word immediately comes to mind when suggesting the introduction of blogs into evidence: hearsay. To understand how we can avoid this pitfall, let us again revisit your car wreck defendant.

Obviously, the first time the defendant's blog is mentioned on cross [examination], opposing counsel will barely leave her seat before shouting a hearsay objection. Assuming that many judges will be unfamiliar with the word blog, let alone its introduction into evidence, it may be wiser to begin this process during discovery rather than at trial.

It would [be] unwise to inquire about blogs within interrogatories or requests for production. This offers an opposing party the opportunity to delete harmful blog entries. At deposition, however, you can either pull up the blog immediately on a laptop or simply call a member of your staff and have him/her save a copy of the blog's archives to his/her computer.

Luckily for you, the defendant was questioned about her blog at an earlier deposition. While proceeding through your usual line of questions, you discovered that the defendant keeps a blog. Not yet knowing what you may find on this blog, yet astutely foreseeing a possible hearsay objection at trial, you proceed with the following questions:

- Does this blog have a name or title? Please spell it.

- What is its full web address?

- How long have you kept this blog?

- To view your blog, does a person need a password?

- If so, who has one?

- If not, does that mean anyone may view it?

- To post on your blog, do you need a password?

- Does anyone else have your blog's password?

- Has anyone else ever posted on your blog?

- If something is written on your blog, you wrote it, is that correct?

The foregoing questions should protect you from any arguments opposing counsel may make regarding origin, author and access, but you are still not completely out of the woods as to hearsay.

Blogs can be utilized during litigation. Imagine knowing that you could have access to the opposing party's personal diary, yet choosing not to look.

In attempting to prove that the defendant ran the red light, you are offering the blog entry as "a statement, other than one made by the declarant while testifying at the trial or hearing, offered in evidence to prove the truth of the matter asserted." By the simplest of definitions, this is hearsay. Thus, to avoid your opponent's objection, you must rely on a hearsay exception.

Here, the defendant's blog entry about running the red light should come in as an admission by a party-opponent: "A statement is not hearsay if . . . [t]he statement is offered against a party and is . . . the party's own statement, in either an individual or a representative capacity." By taking the time to establish origin, author and access during the defendant's deposition, you can now qualify the blog entry as the defendant's "own statement" in an "individual" capacity, thus clearly qualifying under the exception.

Despite the foregoing, what should happen if the judge sustains your opponent's hearsay objection? In terms of the blog's introduction into evidence, you are now blocked. Yet the important portion pertaining to running the red light can still come in to impeach. "A basic rule of evidence provides that prior inconsistent statements may be used to impeach the credibility of a witness." Thus, as the defendant's blog entry remains inconsistent with her previous testimony on direct, it can and should be used to impeach.

The fictional defendant's red light entry represents the mere tip of the iceberg in terms of ways in which blogs can be utilized during litigation. Imagine knowing that you could have access to the opposing party's personal diary, yet choosing not to look.

There Should Be Rules When Bloggers Are Paid for Endorsements

J.D. Lasica

J.D. Lasica is a writer, blogger, and consultant. He is the co-founder and head of Ourmedia.org and president of the Social Media Group, a company that provides media tools to organizations.

It wasn't long ago that bloggers and money had nothing to do with each other. But as the blogosphere exploded into the public consciousness—PubSub estimates there are more than 8 million Weblogs, or online journals—it was inevitable that the captains of commerce would latch onto this increasingly popular form of personal media.

Blogging is growing up. For better, for worse.

It has become common to see advertising on personal blogs. Major corporations such as Microsoft, Nokia and Dr Pepper have launched blogs. . . . Ad-supported blogs such as PaidContent, Weblogs Inc. and Corante have formulated standards for separating commerce from editorial content.

The latest issue thrust before the tribunal of blog opinion: What are the rules when commercial entities offer payments or freebies to get bloggers to write about them?

Several events have sparked a debate about whether an ethical threshold has been crossed: the decision by Marqui, a company in Vancouver, to pay bloggers to mention the company; *Newsweek*'s revelation that a group of 100 technologists in Silicon Valley accepts free products and services in return for word-of-mouth endorsements (or not); and the news that BzzAgent, a 3-year-old Boston company, has enlisted thousands of volunteers to generate buzz for clients' products, sometimes in ethically questionable ways. . . .

Cyberspace and the blogosphere add new wrinkles to the debate. Just how far can marketers go in soliciting blog coverage of their products or services? Does the practice of paying bloggers to blog about a product amount to an advertorial, embedded infomercial or product placement—and does such an arrangement violate the compact of trust between reader and writer? Or is it simply the next logical step in the blogosphere's evolution from hobby to business opportunity? Do different rules apply to journalists who blog?

Stowe Boyd, president of Corante's Weblog network, has been particularly withering in his criticism of the Marqui program, calling the bloggers who agreed to participate "paid shills" and warning that such programs threaten to "turn the blogosphere into a graffiti-laden slum where you won't be able to tell if a blog posting is genuine or a paid message." . . .

Bloggers Have Different Rules than Professional Journalists

Most observers agree on one point: Bloggers and traditional journalists don't play by the same rulebook. Consider the unsparing standards set out in the Society of Professional Journalists' Ethics Code, which instructs journalists to:

- Avoid conflicts of interest, real or perceived.

- Remain free of associations and activities that may compromise integrity or damage credibility.

- Refuse gifts, favors, fees, free travel and special treatment, and shun secondary employment, political involvement, public office and service in community organizations if they compromise journalistic integrity.

- Deny favored treatment to advertisers and special interests and resist their pressure to influence news coverage.

- Be wary of sources offering information for favors or money . . .

Bloggers sometimes act as journalists, but they uniformly say they hew to different standards than professional journalists. "The idea that there has to be a Chinese wall is an industrial-era notion that doesn't take into account the cottage media era we live in," said Mitch Ratcliffe, a veteran tech journalist and blogger. "When I am blogging and I am both publisher and editor, I'm playing by different rules, and there is, across the blogosphere, an evolving set of mores that will never become hard and fast rules for all bloggers."

Bloggers who take money or other graft and, as a result, write biased, uncritical flattery about people, products, ideas, companies, etc., will ultimately lose their credibility.

While they may not have a rulebook, bloggers have evolved a loose-knit set of general tenets. These principles seem to be widely held:

- Disclose, disclose, disclose. Transparency—of actions, motives and financial considerations—is the golden rule of the blogosphere.

- Follow your passions. Blog about topics you care deeply about.

- Be honest. Write what you believe.

- Trust your readers to form their own judgments and conclusions.

- Reputation is the principal currency of cyberspace. Maintain your independence and integrity—lost trust is difficult to regain.

Others have come up with their own formulations. . . . But as Ratcliffe suggests, the blogger's penchant for independence means that even these guidelines may be trumped by an even higher law: Don't impose your rules on me.

People Are Experimenting

"It is still early in the evolution of the Internet, and there is no one true way," [Web designer and blogger Alan] Herrell said.

"The blogosphere runs on customs and norms—on what the community feels is acceptable," adds Steve Rubel, vice president of a New York public relations firm and proprietor of the popular Micropersuasion blog. "It's so early that people are experimenting with different types of marketing models. Eventually, someone will cross the line and the community will police itself."

The latest wrangle over blog ethics began in November [2004] when Marqui, which sells communication management services for automating Web sites, announced its experimental program. The company was seeking to increase awareness of its brand among influential members of the software developer community.

"Our original fear was that this would destroy the whole concept of the free and open blogosphere," said Stephen King, Marqui's CEO and president. "But we decided it could be done if the right safeguards were put in place."

Under the program, disclosure of the bloggers' relationship with Marqui is encouraged. Bloggers are required to publish the Marqui icon and mention Marqui in a blog post at least once a week, but they're free to speak their minds and write anything, positive or negative. They're also free to blog directly about the company's products or pursue a different angle. In return, they receive $800 a month. The initial round of three-month contracts expires [in February 2005].

"We wanted to make certain that this would not be an advertorial, the kind of unscrupulous arrangement where it's unspoken who is paying for what," King said. "We don't tell bloggers what to write. We're doing this to get a conversation started, and we want the right to participate in that debate."

Each of the bloggers headed off in different directions. Ratcliffe declined to write about Marqui's products, instead focusing his blog posts on the implications of the paying-bloggers program itself. [Eric] Rice donated $1,000 of his proceeds to the podcasting community. [Robin] Good decided not to accept a $50 commission for each product lead that his blog generated.

Wrote Good: "I have a radical vision where publishers will choose their sponsors rather the other way around. I know, it may appear crazy, but that is what I am seeing now. I also see a near-coming future where I will be able to personally select the companies/products/services I want to endorse because they fully represent my spirit both in terms of product value as well as in terms of company vision, strategy and attitude.". . .

Disclosure of the payment arrangement between client and blogger ought to be mandatory, not optional—for both parties' sakes.

Some Bloggers Receive Products or Services

Om Malik, a blogger, author and tech reporter for *Business 2.0* magazine, laid into the Silicon Valley [SV] 100 when it was disclosed that 100 influential members of the Bay Area's tech community are periodically offered products or services—or schwag, as Malik terms it—to tout or not tout as they please. . . .

Chris Shipley, an SV100 member who organizes NetworkWorld's DEMO conferences, said, "You need to differentiate between paid shills, product placements and product reviews. Many companies are effectively using bloggers to review their products and these bloggers are doing fair and frank reviews. This is a practice not unlike product reviews in traditional media channels.

"Bloggers who take money or other graft and, as a result, write biased, uncritical flattery about people, products, ideas, companies, etc., will ultimately lose their credibility, and along with it their readership and influence," she adds.

Malik remains unconvinced. "I am going to selectively monitor and remove the feeds of some of bloggers among the schwag set. You don't accept corporate schwag—you write about a product and you ship it back." . . .

While blog advertising has become standard practice, Boyd said, "It starts to get cheesy when the blogger is not necessarily writing entries based on his passions, interests and insights. He's being influenced to put things into his blog because he's being paid to do it. That violates a basic operating principle of the blogosphere. This isn't carved in stone or brought down from the mountaintop on tablets, but the fact that an advertiser is paying you to write about them means that you're handing over your editorial decision-making and you're selling that off. And I think that's wrong." . . .

Blogs Do Not Mislead Readers

King believes that what Marqui is doing falls squarely within the boundaries of ethical behavior. "In the traditional media market, the advertorial is deliberately meant to mislead. It's designed to look like it's part of the newspaper or magazine. We're not doing that. You know what you're getting.

"We all know that influence happens at publications," he added. "So we can't sit here and say, 'Look how pure the real journalists are.' If you advertise in a trade publication, you'll have an influence on whether your company might get mentioned, even if you have no influence on what or how it gets mentioned. The way newspapers handle that is church and state: The advertising people don't influence the writers or editors. But if there's just one person, you can't have a wall because the blogger is taking our money as an ad person and he's also serving as an amateur journalist by writing whatever he wants. But the same code of ethics applies."

That's true, to some extent. But credible publications always demarcate advertorial from editorial content. . . . All reputable publishers require that such content be set off in a different typeface, and they put out the word that their covers and content are not for sale. In other words, you don't need to read the fine print to know you've just read an ad. But Ratcliffe makes the important point that with advertorials, the advertiser controls the content of the message—something that doesn't happen with the paid-bloggers program. . . .

Rubel, the Manhattan marketing executive, said the current advertising landscape is filled with "256 shades of gray," and notes that corporations that have ventured into the blogosphere have generally stumbled, as when Dr Pepper/Seven Up enlisted six teen bloggers to write about a new flavored milk drink called Raging Cow without mentioning their ties to the company; Mazda tried to launch a viral marketing campaign with a fake blog; Warner Bros. began posting blog comments with gushing praise for new WB bands; and McDonald's created a fake Lincolnfry blog as part of an ad campaign.

But Rubel saw many opportunities for new ad models as long as they keep faith with the reader. "I could see bloggers signing major endorsement deals," he said. Why not have Adobe pay the author of a Photoshop book to blog about best practices? Why shouldn't Microsoft give out 500 free copies of the Tablet PC to movers and shakers in the tech world, no strings attached? . . .

Some Suggested Guidelines

Blogs are not newspapers with the same traditions and set of reader expectations. It may be that the Marqui program needs only a bit of fine-tuning. Here are some suggestions:

First, disclosure of the payment arrangement between client and blogger ought to be mandatory, not optional—for both parties' sakes.

If bloggers are paid by a corporation to write about the company, they're no longer acting as amateur journalists.

Second, now that the initial experimental phase is over, the content needs to be demarcated in a consistent way. Liz Lawley has blazed the trail smartly, adding a "sponsored content" label as part of the headline and a box around each sponsored post. (Ratcliffe points out that half the people who read his posts never visit his site but receive the content through RSS feeds—hence the need for a text disclaimer as well as a visual cue.) Even Corante permits sponsored content—for example, Jabber pays people to blog on Corante when attending a conference—but the blog entries are set off so they're clearly differentiated from the rest of the site's content.

Third, bloggers should not be added or dropped based on positive coverage they've provided or based on whether they're willing to write editorial product reviews (favorable or unfavorable).

Fourth, and finally, let's get something straight. If bloggers are paid by a corporation to write about the company, they're no longer acting as amateur journalists. Journalists cannot and do not accept payments from sources.

Bloggers, on the other hand, are free to do so, and it's up to each reader to decide how to judge that. "If you're a blogger or writer, OK, take the money," Rubel said. "But understand that you've crossed a line with some readers."

Just don't call yourself a journalist when you're cashing that check.

Web Resources

Blog Herald www.blogherald.com The longest-standing source of blog-related news, founded in 2003. In addition to daily news about the blogosphere, it contains editorials, reviews, and tutorials.

Blogger www.blogger.com One of the major blog hosting services. It is owned and operated by Google and is free.

Blogger's Choice Awards http://bloggerschoiceawards.com Allows users to vote for the best blog of the year in many different categories.

Bloggers Blog www.bloggersblog.com News about blogging trends, plus extensive resources such as lists of blog directories, blog search engines, tips, FAQs, and a forum.

Blogging Mommies www.bloggingmommies.com "Moms from around the world sharing their lives one post at a time."

Bloggy Award www.bloggyaward.com Reviews blogs and gives awards based on their scores in five categories: Visual Aesthetics, User Friendliness, Reading Enjoyment, Useful Info, and Overall Experience.

Bloglines www.bloglines.com A free online service for searching, subscribing, creating, and sharing news feeds, blogs and rich Web content. It allows readers to search for, read and share updates from their favorite news feed or blog, regardless of its authoring technology, at a single site. This content can also be accessed from handheld computers and mobile phones.

Blogossary www.blogossary.com A useful glossary of terms connected with blogging.

CyberJournalist www.cyberjournalist.net A news and resource site that focuses on how the Internet, convergence, and new technologies are changing the media. It offers tips, news, and commentary about online journalism, citizens' media, digital storytelling, converged news operations, and using the Internet as a reporting tool.

Daily Blog Tips www.dailyblogtips.com Tips on ways of improving blogs and promoting them in order to get more readers.

FeedBurner www.feedburner.com Tools for blog syndication and traffic analysis. A blogger can get code to post that enables readers to subscribe easily through either a news reader or e-mail and to provide statistics about how many people are visiting the blog.

Google Blog Search http://blogsearch.google.com A search engine that works just like Google Web searching, except that only blogs are searched (not all blogs are included in Google Web search results, and even if they do appear, they are mixed with results from other types of sites so that most fall low on the list). Also, the blog search offers the ability to specify a much shorter time range than regular Google searching does; for instance, the search can be limited to content posted within the last hour.

LiveJournal www.livejournal.com One of the major blog hosting services.

Media Bloggers Association (MBA) www.mediabloggers.org A nonpartisan organization dedicated to promoting, protecting, and educating its members; supporting the development of "blogging" or "citizen journalism" as a distinct form of media; and helping to extend the power of the press, with all the rights and responsibilities that entails, to every citizen. Its site contains news pertaining to blogging and the personal blog of its president.

Technorati www.technorati.com The Internet's primary blog search engine. As of March 2008 it was tracking 112.8 million blogs and over 250 million pieces of tagged social media. Its site has daily lists of the most popular blogs and offers the ability to search all blogs by topic or keyword. Individuals can indicate their favorite blogs and can easily see what other blogs have linked to their own.

TypePad www.typepad.com One of the major blog hosting services.

Your Guide to Weblogs http://weblogs.about.com Extensive information about blogging from About.com, including how-to guides, blog tool information, blogging ethics, FAQs, and much more.

WordPress http://wordpress.com One of the major blog hosting services.

Bibliography

Books

Nasrin Alavi

We Are Iran: The Persian Blogs. New York: Soft Skull, 2005.

Jerome Armstrong

Crashing the Gate: Netroots, Grassroots, and the Rise of People-Powered Politics. White River Junction, VT: Chelsea Green, 2006.

Aaron Barlow

Blogging America: The New Public Sphere. Westport, CT: Praeger, 2007.

Axel Bruns and Joanne Jacobs, eds.

Uses of Blogs. New York: Peter Lang, 2006.

Stephen D. Cooper

Watching the Watchdog: Bloggers as the Fifth Estate. Spokane, WA: Marquette, 2006.

Richard Davis

Politics Online: Blogs, Chatrooms, and Discussion Groups in America. New York: Routledge, 2005.

Dan Gillmor

We the Media: Grassroots Journalism by the People, for the People. Sebastopol, CA: O'Reilly, 2004.

John W. Gosney

Blogging for Teens. Boston: Thomson Course Technology, 2004.

Hugh Hewitt

Blog: Understanding the Information Reformation That's Changing Your World. Nashville: Nelson, 2005.

Brad Hill   *Blogging for Dummies*. Hoboken, NJ: Wiley, 2006.

Andrew Keen   *The Cult of the Amateur: How Today's Internet Is Killing Our Culture*. New York: Doubleday/Currency, 2007.

Michael Keren   *Blogosphere: The New Political Arena*. Lanham, MD: Lexington, 2006.

David Kline and Dan Burstein   *Blog! How the Newest Media Revolution Is Changing Politics, Business, and Culture*. New York: CDS, 2005.

Peter Kuhns and Adrienne Crew   *Blogosphere: Best of Blogs*. Indianapolis: Que, 2006.

Nat McBride and Jamie Carson   *Teach Yourself Blogging*. New York: McGraw-Hill, 2006.

Barbara O'Brien   *Blogging America: Political Discourse in a Digital Nation*. Wilsonville, OR: William James, 2004.

Will Richardson   *Blogs, Wikis, Podcasts, and Other Powerful Web Tools for Classrooms*. Thousand Oaks, CA: Corwin, 2006.

Aliza Risdahl   *The Everything Blogging Book: Publish Your Ideas, Get Feedback, and Create Your Own Worldwide Network*. Avon, MA: Adam Media, 2006.

John Rodzvilla, ed.   *We've Got Blog: How Weblogs Are Changing Our Culture*. Cambridge, MA: Perseus, 2002.

Lynne Rominger   *Extraordinary Blogs and Ezines*. New York: Franklin Watts, 2006.

Robert Scoble	*Naked Conversations: How Blogs Are Changing the Way Businesses Talk with Customers.* Hoboken, NJ: Wiley, 2006.
Biz Stone	*Who Let the Blogs Out? A Hyperconnected Peek at the World of Weblogs.* New York: St. Martin's, 2004.
Mark Tremayne, ed.	*Blogging, Citizenship, and the Future of Media.* New York: Routledge, 2006.
Bob Walsh	*Clear Blogging: How People Blogging Are Changing the World and How You Can Join Them.* Berkeley, CA: Apress, 2007.
David Warlick	*Classroom Blogging: A Teacher's Guide to the Blogosphere.* Morrisville, NC: Lulu, 2005.

Periodicals

Stephen Armstrong	"Bloggers for Hire: The Days of Genuine 'Citizen-Generated' Media May Be Numbered," *New Statesman*, August 28, 2006.
Robert W. Ashmore and Brian M. Herman	"Abuse in Cyberspace: School Lawyers on Dealing with Questionable Actions in the Blogosphere by School Staff and Students," *School Administrator*, May 2006.
Dean Barnett	"Bad Company: Is the Left-Wing Blogosphere a Growing Political Force or an Electoral Burden?" *Weekly Standard*, June 15, 2006.

Elizabeth Bird — "Blogging the Kidlitosphere," *Horn Book Magazine*, May/June 2007.

Carolyn Kleiner Butler — "Blogging Their Way Through Academe," *U.S. News & World Report*, April 10, 2006.

Jen Christensen — "Jeff vs. the Bloggers," *Advocate*, May 10, 2005.

Barbara Curtis — "Mom-to-Mom Blogging," *Christian Science Monitor*, April 3, 2007.

Geeta Dayal — "What If Professors Could Lecture 24-7? Blog Culture Invades Academia," *Village Voice*, Education Supplement, Spring 2005.

Celina R. DeLeon — "The Segregated Blogosphere: With More People of Color Blogging than Ever Before, Race Still Gets Pushed to the Back," *Colorlines Magazine*, March/April 2007.

Mary Branham Dusenberry — "Blogging Government," *State News*, September 2006.

Jonathan Freedland — "The Blogosphere Risks Putting Off Everyone but Point-Scoring Males," *Guardian* (UK), April 11, 2007.

David Glenn — "A Bark-and-Byte Battle over Campaign Finance," *Chronicle of Higher Education*, April 21, 2006.

Michael Gorman — "Revenge of the Blog People!" *Library Journal*, February 15, 2005.

Lev Grossman   "Blogs Have Their Day," *Time*, December 27, 2004.

Lev Grossman   "Meet Joe Blog," *Time*, June 13, 2004.

Kevin W. Holland   "Welcome to the Blogosphere," *Association Management*, May 2005.

Shirley Duglin   "Us versus Them," *Information Today*,
Kennedy   April 2007.

Elizabeth Kirby   "Student Blogs Mark a New Frontier
and Brenda Kaillo   for School Discipline," *Education Digest*, January 2007.

David   "Why There's No Escaping the Blog,"
Kirkpatrick,   *Fortune*, January 24, 2005.
Daniel Roth, and
Oliver Ryan

Josh Larson   "The Emergence of the Weather Blog," *Weatherwise*, January/February 2007.

*American   "Mattering in the School Blogo-
Libraries*   sphere," May 2007.

Keith McPherson   "School Library Blogging," *Teacher Librarian*, June 2006.

Richard   "A Day in the Life, Subatomically
Monastersky   Speaking," *Chronicle of Higher Education*, July 1, 2005.

William Powers   "The Massless Media," *Atlantic Monthly*, January/February 2005.

*San Francisco   "Blogging Prosecutors Raise Some
Chronicle*   Eyebrows," February 25, 2007.

Corilyn Shropshire	"Most Americans Who Keep Blogs Do So Under Assumed Names," *Pittsburgh Post-Gazette*, November 2, 2006.
Philip Weiss	"Mondoweiss, Chapter One," *American Conservative*, June 4, 2007.
Steve Yahn and Jake Whitney	"Defending Blogs," *Editor & Publisher*, August 1, 2006.

Index